Who's Your County Named For?

And Other Hoosier County Facts

Glenda S. Shull

Who's Your County Named For? And Other Hoosier County Facts
by Glenda S. Shull

Managing Editor: Mimi Kilic

Photo Credits: 32, George Rogers Clark National Historical Park; 35, Amax Coal Industries, Inc.; 40, Wyandotte Cave, Division of Forestry, Indiana Department of Natural Resources; 57 (upper), Allen County Public Library; 57, Missouri Historical Society; 58 (upper) Auburn-Cord-Duesenberg Museum; 58 (lower), Ball Corporation; 79, 104 (lower), 163, Indiana Historical Society; 80, The New York Public Library; 86, 98, 103, 104 (upper), 160, 205, Indiana State Library; 164, Lincoln Boyhood National Memorial; 164, Porter County; 189, Indian Historical Society and Glenn A. Black Laboratory of Archaelogy.

ISBN: 0-938682-20-2

Published and distributed by River Road Publications, Inc.
Spring Lake, Michigan 49456

Contents

Introduction.   5
Adams County.   7
Allen County.   10
Bartholomew County.   13
Benton County.   15
Blackford County.   17
Boone County   19
Brown County   22
Carroll County   24
Cass County   26
Clark County.   29
Gallery.   32
Clay County   33
Clinton County   36
Crawford County.   38
Daviess County   41
Dearborn County   43
Decatur County   45
DeKalb County   47
Delaware County   49
Dubois County   51
Elkhart County   53
Fayette County.   55
Gallery.   57
Floyd County   59
Fountain County   61
Franklin County   63
Fulton County.   65
Gibson County   67
Grant County   69
Greene County   71
Hamilton County.   73
Hancock County.   75
Harrison County.   77
Gallery   80
Hendricks County.   81
Henry County   83
Howard County   85
Huntington County   87
Jackson County   89
Jasper County   92
Jay County   94

Jefferson County   96
Jennings County   99
Johnson County   101
Gallery   103
Knox County   105
Kosciusko County.   107
La Grange   109
Lake County.   111
LaPorte County.   113
Lawrence County   115
Madison County.   117
Marion County.   119
Marshall County.   121
Martin County.   123
Miami County.   125
Monroe County.   127
Montgomery County   129
Morgan County.   131
Newton County.   133
Noble County.   135
Ohio County.   137
Orange County   139
Owen County   141
Parke County   143
Perry County   145
Pike County.   147
Porter County.   149
Posey County.   151
Pulaski County   153
Putnam County   155
Randolph County.   157
Ripley County.   159
Rush County   161
Gallery   163
St. Joseph County.   165
Scott County   167
Shelby County   169
Spencer County   171
Starke County   173
Steuben County   175
Sullivan County   177
Switzerland County.   179

Tippecanoe County. 181
Tipton County. 184
Union County. 186
Vanderburgh County 188
Vermillion County 190
Vigo County 192
Wabash County 194
Warren County 196
Warrick County 198
Washington County. 200
Wayne County 203
Wells County. 206
White County. 209
Whitley County. 211
County Charts 213
Glossary 217
Index. 222

Introduction

When Indiana became a state in 1816, it had only fifteen counties. Nearly all of these counties were located in the southernmost part of the state where most of Indiana's earliest white settlers came to live. The boundaries of these first counties were not all exactly the same as they are today. For example, Knox County, located in southern Indiana, touched the northern boundaries of the state! Gradually, many counties were carved out of Knox. By 1844 all of Indiana's 92 counties had been formed.

At the beginning of each chapter there are dates showing when that county was organized. Because many changes took place in those early years, a county was sometimes organized more than one time. In this book, the dates given are the last dates the county was organized.

It may seem strange to you that many of the people Indiana's counties are named for never even visited Indiana. This is not so strange, however, when you remember that names were given to counties when the state was very new. Only a few people had the chance to become leading Hoosiers, a nickname for Indiana citizens.

It is also important to remember that many Indiana settlers came from the eastern United States. Their heroes had fought in the American Revolution or were important government leaders. Hoosiers, like many other Americans, were glad to have a chance to honor the people who helped form the great United States!

Adams County

Named for: John Quincy Adams
Date organized: 1835

When settlers in a part of northeastern Indiana chose a name for their county, they must have thought about the nation's outstanding leaders. They selected the name of a man who was serving in the U. S. **Congress** and who had already been President of the young United States. That man was John Quincy Adams.

John Quincy Adams was born in Braintree (now Quincy), Massachusetts, on July 11, 1767. Although John Quincy was only six years old when the **Boston Tea Party** took place, his whole family was caught up in the excitement of the **American Revolution**. His father, John Adams, helped organize an army to fight for the thirteen colonies. Mr. Adams so believed in the American cause that the family gave its valuable **pewter** spoons to be melted down into bullets.

Young John received much of his early education from his gifted mother and father. During the American Revolution, his father stayed in Boston. John helped his mother manage the farm. By the age of nine, young John was part of the war effort. He carried letters and news between Braintree and Boston.

The Adams family wanted John Quincy to have a good education. When he was eleven, young John went with his father to

Europe and attended school in France. At the age of twelve he entered a Dutch university. And by the age of fourteen he could read and write six languages!

John Quincy continued his education in America. He enrolled in Harvard College and graduated after only two years. Then he opened a law office in Boston.

The year 1797 was an important one for John Quincy. His father, John Adams, became President of the United States. John Quincy married Louisa Johnson. The couple later had three children. One of them was named George Washington Adams in honor of the first President of the United States.

John Quincy held many jobs in government. He served as a minister, or representative, of the United States in such countries as the Netherlands, Great Britain, and Russia. President James Madison* chose him as **Secretary of State**. In 1825 John Quincy Adams himself became President of the United States.

John Quincy Adams combined hard work with exercise. He walked several miles each day. He also liked to take early morning swims in the Potomac River in Washington, D.C. One story says that as he swam to shore one morning he found a woman reporter sitting on his clothes. She said she would not give him the clothes unless he allowed her to write a story about him. He, of course, had no choice but to agree!

When Indiana settlers decided to name a county after him, John Quincy Adams had finished his term as President. But he had not retired. The citizens of Massachusetts had elected him to serve in the U. S. **House of Representatives**. He continued his years of service there until 1848, when he died of a stroke.

See Madison County.

About Adams County

Land and resources: Adams County has mostly level land with many farms and some hardwood forests, which include oak, ash, elm, hickory, and cottonwood trees. The county has natural resources such as sand, gravel, and **limestone.** It also has deposits of **peat**, oil and gas. The Wabash River flows through the county.

People and their work: About 41 percent of the county's workers have jobs in factories. Others run stores or have professional jobs, working as lawyers, doctors, or teachers. Many of the county's people are farmers who raise dairy cattle and poultry and grow crops such as oats and winter wheat.

Facts to remember about Adams County: A number of Amish people live on the farms here in a style of life that differs very little from that of their grandparents and great-grandparents. The Amish travel by horse and buggy. Their homes have no running water or electricity for lights, cooking, or television. They choose this simple way of life because of their religion and ideas about how people should live.

Allen County

Named for: John Allen
Date organized: 1835

John Allen was born on December 30, 1772, to a pioneer family in Rockbridge County, Virginia. When John was eight years old, the family moved to Kentucky, where they lived in **frontier** settlements.The Allens were one of the first families in the Kentucky wilderness to build their log home outside the walls of a fort.

The wilderness was John's school until he was twelve. He then began school in Bardstown, Kentucky. In 1791 he took up the study of law in Virginia. Four years later he returned to Kentucky and opened a law practice. As time went on, John became involved in politics. In 1799 he married Jane Logan.

When the **War of 1812** began, John Allen was a **senator** in Kentucky. He immediately became a soldier, raising an army of Kentucky volunteers. When Allen and his men learned that some Potawatomi Indians were planning to attack Fort Wayne, they marched to the area. When they arrived, the area outside the fort had already been attacked. Colonel Allen took charge of destroying the nearby Indian villages.

In January, 1813, Allen and 110 men headed north toward Detroit. They joined other American troops in an attempt to recapture Fort Detroit, which had fallen to the British. Near what is now Monroe, Michigan, the British and a large army of their Indian friends attacked the Americans. In the struggle, no American commander's orders could be heard. The American soldiers scattered in all directions. Colonel Allen, wounded in the thigh, sat on a log shouting orders hopelessly until he was killed by an Indian. His body was never found. Allen was only one of many Americans who lost their lives at the battle known as the "River Raisin Massacre."

Since John Allen's body was not found, his wife never gave up hope that he was still alive. She set a candle in the window each night, hoping for his return. Finally, eight years later, she herself died. The people of Fort Wayne did not forget Allen either. Remembering how he had come to the aid of settlers in their area, they chose his name for their county.

About Allen County

Land and resources: Much of Allen County's land is level, with some gently rolling hills in the northern area. About 70 percent of the land is used for farming, and there are forests of oak, hickory, elm, ash, and other hardwoods. Allen county also has natural resources of oil and gas, sand, gravel, limestone, and peat. The Maumee, St. Joseph, and St. Marys rivers all meet in Allen County at Fort Wayne.

People and their work: Many of the county's people live and work in the Fort Wayne area. They have jobs in offices, stores, and schools. Others work in factories that produce such items as electrical machines and equipment, tires, and transportation equipment. Farmers in the county raise such crops as winter wheat, oats, and soybeans.

Facts to remember about Allen County: Fort Wayne was once known as Kekionga, headquarters of the Miami Indians in the 1700s. General Anthony Wayne destroyed the village in 1794 as the Americans began to move into the **Northwest Territory.** He then built a fort that became one of the main settlements in the Indiana Territory.

John Chapman, better known as Johnny Appleseed, is buried in Fort Wayne. Johnny traveled on foot through much of the Midwest, planting apple seeds that grew into fine trees. Apples are still an important fruit crop in the state.

In the 1800s the people of Indiana planned and built a canal that stretched from the Maumee River to the Wabash River near Terre Haute. Called the Wabash and Erie Canal, it began in Allen County at Fort Wayne. The canal connected Lake Erie with the Wabash by way of the Maumee River.

An old drawing showing Fort Wayne in 1812.

Bartholomew County

Named for: Joseph Bartholomew
Date organized: 1821

Joseph Bartholomew, a military hero, was born on March 15, 1766, in New Jersey. When he was two years old, his family moved to Pennsylvania. As soon as he was old enough to tote a rifle, Joseph joined the **Colonial army**. During the American Revolution, he began his lifetime job of fighting Indians.

Joseph came to the Northwest Territory with the army of General Anthony Wayne.* It was Wayne's job to end the Indian attacks on American settlers in the territory. When that job was over, Joseph went with a group of settlers to Kentucky. There he became a scout and spy for the United States.

When the Indian people gave up their land in what is now southern Indiana, Joseph Bartholomew moved to Clark County. There he was a lieutenant colonel in an Indiana militia, or group of citizens who served as soldiers when necessary. This militia fought in the well-known Battle of Tippecanoe.** During the Battle of Tippecanoe, Joseph became known as a skillful leader. The night before battle he wisely ordered the soldiers to sleep with their weapons. As he made his rounds the next morning, the Indians attacked. With courage and coolness, Joseph led a charge of soldiers and stopped the main force of Indians. Because of his bravery, he was promoted to the rank of general.

One of the soldiers who served under Joseph Bartholomew at the Battle of Tippecanoe was John Tipton.*** Tipton later introduced a bill in the state government to form a new county and name it Bartholomew County. The bill, of course, passed.

Joseph Bartholomew served in both houses of the Indiana **legislature**. He and his family then moved on to Illinois. There Bartholomew returned to his old career of Indian fighter and took part in the **Black Hawk War**. Bartholomew died in 1840.

See Wayne County.
*** See Tippecanoe County.*
**** See Tipton County.*

About Bartholomew County

<u>Land and resources:</u> There are low hills in the northern and eastern parts of the county. In the central areas, the land is level. There are steep hills along the county's western edge. Some of the land is covered with hardwood forests. The county also has limestone, sand, and gravel deposits.

<u>People and their work:</u> A large number of the county's people work in factories. Others work in stores or have jobs as doctors, teachers, and lawyers. The county also has many farmers, who raise crops such as winter wheat, corn, and soybeans.

<u>Facts to remember about Bartholomew County:</u> The city of Columbus has become well known for its modern buildings designed by famous **architects**. The city has unusual schools and handsome churches. Some of its old buildings have been redone and are as beautiful now as they were a century ago.

Benton County

Named for: Thomas Hart Benton
Date organized: 1840

Thomas Hart Benton, a lawyer and politician, was born near Hillsborough, North Carolina, on March 14, 1782. His father died when Thomas was only eight years old. He was raised by his mother, who moved the Benton family to Tennessee. There Thomas studied law and began a law practice in Nashville.

Thomas served as a colonel and aide under Andrew Jackson* in the War of 1812. As a result, Thomas and the famous Jackson became close friends. But the friendship was broken by a fight between Jackson and Thomas Benton's brother.

After the War of 1812, Benton moved to St. Louis, Missouri. There he worked as a lawyer and newspaper editor. In 1820 he was elected to serve Missouri in the United States Senate. He held that job for thirty years. During that time Benton renewed his friendship with Jackson and became one of his strong supporters.

As a U.S. Senator, Benton was a champion of the common people. He believed that settlers should be able to move west. He felt that the Indians should be removed so that their lands could be used by white farmers. Benton was also one of the first to call for a railroad that would stretch to the Pacific coast.

Benton lost his Senate seat in the election of 1850 because of his strong belief that the United States should outlaw slavery. He did not live to see the nation broken by the **Civil War**, however. Benton died in 1858.

* See Jackson County.

About Benton County

Land and resources: Level land makes up all of Benton County. In the lowest areas there are marshes and bogs, and there are only a small number of forests compared with other counties in the state. In some areas there are deposits of sand and gravel. Nearly all the land in the county is used for farming.

People and their work: Benton County is made up largely of farms and small towns and has one of the smallest **populations** of all Indiana counties. Many of the farmers raise soybeans and corn, and county leaders say Benton is the soybean capital of the world. Others who live in the county work in businesses that are related to farming, such as selling seeds and farm equipment. A large number of people go to work outside the county.

Facts to remember about Benton County: Many people in the county enjoy crafts and antiques and have built little businesses from these interests.

Blackford County

Named for: Isaac Blackford
Date organized: 1838

Isaac Blackford, like many of Indiana's early citizens, was born in the East. His birthplace was Bound Brook in Somerset County, New Jersey. Isaac was born on November 6, 1786. At sixteen he entered Princeton College and graduated with honors four years later. He then studied law and received his license in 1810.

Isaac moved west soon after receiving his license to practice law. He settled in Ohio, and then moved on to Salem, Indiana. During his first years in Indiana, Isaac held several public offices. In 1816 he was elected to the first state legislature and was chosen **speaker of the house**. He then was appointed a member of the Indiana **Supreme Court**.

During his thirty-five years on the Supreme Court, Isaac played a very important role. He wrote, edited, and published reports of all the decisions, or judgments, made by the Court. His work made up seven large books, which have been used by lawyers for years and years.

Isaac ran for other public offices in his lifetime. He was defeated in races for governor of Indiana and for the U.S. **Senate**. In 1855 he was appointed to the position of judge in Washington, D.C., and he held that job until his death in 1859.

Isaac Blackford's personal life was a sad one. He married Caroline McDonald, but she died when the couple's first child was born. Isaac loved the child, a son, dearly. But tragedy struck again when the boy died in his youth. It was said that Blackford never fully recovered from his grief.

About Blackford County

Land and resources: Most of the land in the county is level, with over 80 percent of it used for farming. The Salamonie River cuts through the northeast corner of the county, and there are some forests with hardwoods such as oak, beech, maple, and ash. The county has deposits of sand, gravel, limestone, and dolomite.

People and their work: Farmers in the county raise crops such as oats and winter wheat. Many of them also raise hogs. A large number of the county's people also work in factories that make such products as automobile parts, special types of paper, and cardboard containers.

Facts to remember about Blackford County: Blackford is one of the four smallest counties in the state and was among the last to be organized.

Boone County

Named for: Daniel Boone
Date organized: 1830

Daniel was born near Reading, Pennsylvania, on November 2, 1734, to Squire Boone and his wife, Sarah. One of eleven children, Daniel had little schooling. But Daniel was not looking for knowledge from books. He loved to hunt, and on his twelfth birthday he received his first rifle.

When Daniel was sixteen his family moved to North Carolina. There he married Rebecca Bryan. Although he tried to settle down to farming, Daniel preferred to make a living by hunting and fur trading.

In 1767 Daniel made his first trip into Kentucky. During the next few years he explored the region while he hunted and trapped. He learned about a path through the **Cumberland Mountains** that later became a route for settlers moving westward. He was also captured by Indians, but later escaped.

Daniel wanted to settle in Kentucky. He led a group of families into the region, but they were attacked by Indians. The Boone's sixteen-year-old son Jamie was killed and scalped, and the families turned back to their homes.

In 1775 Boone again led a group of pioneers west. They marked a path through the forest called the **Wilderness Road.**

The group began three new settlements, one of them called Boonesborough. There was the constant danger of Indian attacks on the settlements, but Boone brought his family there. His wife and daughter became the first white women to live in Kentucky.

In 1778 Daniel was captured by Indians. He pretended to let them adopt him and wash away his white blood. But after five months he escaped. He rushed back to Boonesborough with the news that an attack would soon take place.

As more people came to Boonesborough, Daniel grew restless. He moved into the wilderness, where he again faced Indian attacks. His brother Edward was killed. In another battle, Boone's son Israel was killed.

Daniel Boone spent his later years surveying, hunting, and guiding settlers to new homes. When the Boones lost all their land because of problems with their land claims, they opened a tavern and store. In 1814 the United States Government gave Daniel 850 acres of land as a reward for his services to the country.

Even as an old man, Daniel Boone loved to hunt and trap. He traveled the wilderness lands of Kansas and Missouri. He also volunteered to serve in the War of 1812 but was turned down because of his age. Daniel Boone died in Missouri in the fall of 1820, ten years before the people of Indiana decided to name a county after him. His life's adventures have continued to live, however, as they are retold in books, comics, movies, and on television.

About Boone County

Land and resources: Most of the land in Boone County is level. Over 80 percent of it is used for farming. There are hardwood forests of oak, beech, maple, and ash. The county also has deposits of sand and gravel.

People and their work: Farmers in Boone County grow crops such as soybeans, corn, oats, winter wheat, and hay. They also raise hogs, poultry, and cattle. A large number of people have jobs in health care, law offices, or some type of social work. Many also go to jobs in neighboring counties.

Facts to remember about Boone County: In the early 1900s people from many different parts of the nation and the world visited Lebanon, the county seat, to view the pillars of the new Boone County Courthouse. Each of the 8 columns is 38 feet high and weighs about 40 tons. The pillars were all carved out of single blocks of limestone.

Brown County

Named for: Jacob Jennings Brown
Date organized: 1836

Jacob Brown, a hero of the War of 1812, was born to Quaker parents in Bucks County, Pennsylvania, on May 9, 1775. As a young man, he worked as a **surveyor** in Ohio where much of the land was still a wilderness. In 1798 he settled in New York City where he served as a military secretary to the famous Alexander Hamilton.*

Brown later moved on to Jefferson County, New York. There he bought land and founded a town. He became a judge in the town, which was named Brownville.

When the War of 1812 broke out, Brown fought with the United States against the British. He was put in charge of protecting the New York State frontier. In 1813, after holding off British attacks, he was made a brigadier general. By 1814 he was promoted to major general. He became a hero for his victories at Chippewa, Lundy's Lane (where he was wounded twice), and Fort Erie, all British strongholds in Canada.

After the War of 1812, Brown remained in the U. S. Army. He served as General in Chief from 1821 until his death in 1828.

* *See Hamilton County.*

About Brown County

Land and resources: Brown County is made up of hills and valleys, with only a small part of the land used for farming. There are many acres of forests, which are made up largely of oak, maple, hickory, beech, and birch trees. The county has deposits of limestone and **shale**.

People and their work: Brown County has one of the smallest populations of any county in the state. Many of the county's people work in restaurants, hotels, and stores that serve the many tourists that come to spend time in the area's beautiful parks and forests.

Facts to remember about Brown County: Many artists and craftspeople live and work in Brown County, selling their creations to the county's visitors.

Carroll County

Named for: Charles Carroll
Date organized: 1828

Charles Carroll, a great American patriot, was born in Annapolis, Maryland, on September 20, 1737. His family could trace its background to the early kings of Ireland. Charles's family was also very rich, and they sent him to France for his education. He studied in Jesuit schools and colleges since his family was Roman Catholic. He also studied law in Paris, France, and London, England.

When Charles returned to the colonies in America his father gave him 10,000 acres of land in Maryland. He named his estate Carrollton Manor and was known as Charles Carroll of Carrollton. He was strongly against British rule in America. He also opposed the **Stamp Act** and wrote newspaper stories against British rule. In 1774 he played an important role in Maryland's version of the Boston Tea Party. In this event a shipload of tea was burned in Annapolis. Charles also helped convince Maryland's members in the **Continental Congress** to declare the colonies free and independent states.

In 1776 Charles, along with Benjamin Franklin and Samuel Chase, traveled to Canada. There they tried to urge the Canadians to take part in the American Revolution, but were not successful. Charles went on working for the Revolution. He served as a member in the Continental Congress. He willingly signed the **Declaration of Independence**, although he knew his own fortune would be lost if the Americans did not win the war.

When the colonies became states, Charles turned his energy to the development of Maryland. He helped write Maryland's state **constitution**. He also served as a member of Maryland's senate as well as a United States Senator from Maryland.

Charles Carroll lived longer than any other signer of the Declaration of Independence. In his nineties he dug the first shovelful of dirt when the country's first railroad, the Baltimore and Ohio, was begun.

About Carroll County

Land and resources: Much of the land in Carroll County is level and is used for farming. There are some hardwood forests, which include oak, hickory, and maple trees. The county has limestone, **dolomite**, sand, gravel, peat, and shale deposits. The Wabash River flows through the county.

People and their work: Farmers in the county raise a large number of hogs. They also grow corn, soybeans, oats, and winter wheat. Many of the county's people have jobs in stores, banks, or in the health care fields. Some go to other counties to work.

Facts to remember about Carroll County: In the 1890s a farm in Carroll County was said to have been the first in the nation to grow soybeans, a plant that came from China.

Cass County

Named for: Lewis Cass
Date organized: 1829

Lewis Cass was born in Exeter, New Hampshire, on October 9, 1782. He grew up in a family that was deeply involved in the affairs of the new nation. His father was an Army officer, who continued to serve after the American Revolution. When President George Washington* visited the Cass's hometown of Exeter, Lewis's father, Major Cass, introduced his family to the President. It was a day that Lewis never forgot.

When Lewis's family moved to western Pennsylvania so that Major Cass could be in the army of General Anthony Wayne,** Lewis remained in the East. He attended Phillips Academy, where he became friends with Daniel Webster, who grew up to become a great statesman and speaker. Lewis had a fine education and even became a teacher for a short time. But he longed to move west to Ohio.

In 1800 the Cass family moved to Ohio, then part of the Northwest Territory, and settled down to farm. Lewis worked on the homestead, but also began to study law. By the age of twenty, he earned the right to practice law in Ohio.

Lewis's law career soon turned into a political one. He was elected to serve as county **prosecutor** and then as an Ohio lawmaker. His political career was interrupted, however, by the outbreak of the War of 1812. As colonel of an Ohio regiment, Cass soon found himself in the **Michigan Territory**, where the commander of Fort Detroit surrendered to the British. Lewis was captured by the British, but was later released. He rose to the office of brigadier general. Soon after that he was appointed governor of the Michigan Territory.

For eighteen years Lewis Cass was governor of the Michigan Territory. He explored the region, made treaties with the Indians, and helped build a strong system of education. Before Michigan became a state, Cass left his post to become **Secretary of War** for President Andrew Jackson.*** He also served as **ambassador** to France and a United States Senator from Michigan.

Twice Cass was considered by the Democratic party as a candidate for President. Although he did not achieve the long-lasting fame of his friend Daniel Webster, Lewis Cass was a powerful figure in his time. He was chosen to speak at the opening of the **Wabash and Erie Canal**, the longest canal ever built in North America. It was clear that even though Lewis Cass served the entire nation, the states that had made up the Northwest Territory claimed him as their own.

* See Washington County.
** See Wayne County.
*** See Jackson County.

About Cass County

<u>Land and resources:</u> Much of Cass County has low, rolling hills, especially along the Wabash River, which flows through the middle of the county. The county has deposits of limestone and dolomite, along with sand and gravel. Hardwood forests made up of oak, hickory, beech, and maple are scattered throughout the county.

<u>People and their work:</u> Farmers in Cass County raise corn, soybeans, oats, and hay. More than 30 percent of the county's people work in factories that make such products as car batteries and electrical parts for cars and boats. Others have jobs in recreation areas and in various types of health agencies. Some work in a meat-packing plant that makes meat products from the many hogs raised in the state.

<u>Facts to remember about Cass County:</u> Logansport, the county seat, has also been an important transportation center. The **Michigan Road** ran through it, along with the Wabash and Erie Canal. The first railroad came to Logansport in 1855. By the early 1900s the city was a large railroad center with nearly 3,000 people working on the railroads that stretched out of the county in nine different directions.

Clark County

Named for: George Rogers Clark
Date organized: 1801

A hero of the American Revolution, George Rogers Clark was born near Charlottesville, Virginia, on November 19, 1752. As a young man he became a surveyor and worked in the large region between the colonies and the Mississippi River. The Indians there were angry because Americans tried to move in and settle on Indian land. To protect their lands, the Indians bought guns at British trading posts and often attacked any Americans who tried to come into the region.

When the American Revolution began, George Clark knew that the many Indian tribes in the large area where he had been surveying would join the British and fight against the Americans. Clark decided it would be important for the Americans to capture the small British posts in this territory even though they were far from the colonies. This would make it difficult for the Indians to get guns.

Clark took his plan to the leaders of Virginia, who at that time claimed that much of the land west of the colonies belonged to them. They supported Clark's ideas, made him a military commander, and gave him money for supplies. In June, 1778, he began to march west with an army of 175 men.

Clark traveled as far as the Mississippi River. There he captured forts at Kaskaskia and Cahokia in what is now Illinois. He also took Fort Sackville in what is now Vincennes, Indiana. Leaving a few men at Vincennes, Clark went back to Kaskaskia.

A British commander at Fort Detroit, Henry Hamilton, was alarmed by Clark's victories. Hamilton, whom Clark and his men called "the hair buyer" because he was said to pay Indians for bringing him American scalps, marched to Vincennes with a large army and quickly recaptured the fort. Since there were only a few supplies to last through the winter months, Hamilton sent many of his soldiers back to Fort Detroit while he remained at Fort Sackville.

Clark learned about Hamilton's takeover of Fort Sackville through a man named Francis Vigo.* Although it was unusual to attack in winter, Clark decided his only chance to defeat Hamilton was to take him by surprise. Early in February, 1779, Clark and his men began a 180-mile march from Kaskaskia to Vincennes. The march was especially hard because of early flooding. They had to build canoes and often wade through freezing water. As they neared Vincennes, they also ran out of food.

But Clark was successful in surprising Hamilton. Certain that he was safe until spring, Hamilton did not expect trouble. He did not know about Clark's attack until he heard the sound of the guns. By then it was too late. Clark was the victor and a great hero. He had greatly weakened British power in the west.

Clark went on to fight in the American Revolution. He helped defeat the British near St. Louis. He also defeated the Shawnee Indians near today's Chillicothe, Ohio.

Clark received a large amount of land in payment for his service in the American Revolution. This land included the present Clark, Scott, and Floyd counties. He founded several communities and also worked as an Indian commissioner to help the young United States gain land through treaties with the Indians. A severe burn to one of his legs forced him to stay in a wheelchair until his death in 1818.

* See Vigo County.

About Clark County

Land and resources: Located along the Ohio River, Clark County is made up largely of hilly land. Part of it is covered with hardwood forests of oak and hickory. The county also has deposits of oil and gas, limestone, sand, gravel, and dolomite.

People and their work: A large number of people work in the county's factories, which build such interesting products as river barges and baseball bats. Many residents are also employed in neighboring counties. Farmers in the area raise tobacco, soybeans, corn, oats, and hay. Some farmers also grow strawberries.

Facts to remember about Clark County: Along the banks of the Ohio River at Clarksville are fossil beds, part of a **coral reef** which is about 375 million years old. The amazing formations bring many tourists and scientists to the area.

The British commander Henry Hamilton (in the uniform) surrenders to George Rogers Clark at Fort Sackville during the American Revolutionary War. The old drawing below shows Fort Sackville as it looked in 1778.

Clay County

Named for: Henry Clay
Date organized: 1825

Henry Clay was born in Hanover County, Virginia, on April 12, 1777, just when the American Revolution had begun. His father died when Henry was four years old. When the Clays and their friends returned from the funeral, they found that British soldiers had entered their home, eaten the food for the funeral meal, and taken everything of value.

Henry had little formal education and in his youth worked on his family's farm and in a mill. He once heard Patrick Henry* give a speech and decided that he, too, would become an **orator**. He practiced every chance he could.

When Henry's mother remarried, the family moved to Richmond, Virginia's capital. Although the family soon moved on to Kentucky, Henry stayed in Richmond. There he had a job as a clerk who copied papers in a court office. But his greatest interest was in public speaking. He and several other young men formed a speaking club.

The people Henry worked with were impressed with him and helped him become a lawyer. Eventually Henry moved to Kentucky, where he became wealthy by accepting land as payment for his law services.

33

In 1803 Henry Clay was elected to the state legislature in Kentucky and began his long career as a **politician** and orator. He served as a United States Senator, Speaker of the House of Representatives, and Secretary of State under John Quincy Adams.** He ran for President three times, but was defeated each time.

Through his political skill and fine speaking ability, Henry Clay played an important part in the United States government in the first half of the 1800s. He was known as the **Great Compromiser** because he was good at finding solutions to problems that were tearing the young nation apart. At the same time he often took stands that made him unpopular.

In his early twenties, Henry Clay married Lucretia Hart, and the couple had eleven children. They owned a beautiful farm in Kentucky with many horses. The family also owned as many as fifty slaves. Although Clay took part in the early arguments over slavery, he died in 1852, nearly ten years before the outbreak of the Civil War. His will provided for the freeing of his slaves.

* *See Henry County.*
** *See Adams County.*

About Clay County

Land and resources: The land in Clay County varies from very level to slightly hilly, especially in the south. About three fourths of the land is used for farming. There are hardwood forests of oak, black hickory, and honey locust. The county has deposits of oil and gas, limestone, **sandstone**, clay, shale, and coal.

People and their work: Farmers in the county raise corn and soybeans. Many of the county's people work outside the county. Others have jobs in stores, coal mines, and industries that make such products as brick and tile.

Facts to remember about Clay County: Clay County has some of the state's richest coal deposits, and mining has been important there since the 1850s. Some of the **strip mines** have been made into lakes and recreational areas.

A dragline crane works a strip, or surface mine located along the borders of Clay and Vigo counties.

Clinton County

Named for: De Witt Clinton
Date organized: 1830

In the first half of the 1800s, Americans were very interested in building canals in many different parts of the nation. The country's most famous canal opened in 1825. It was the Erie Canal, and its founder was a man named De Witt Clinton. When the people of Indiana thought about important Americans to name their counties after in 1830, it was not surprising that they thought of Clinton.

De Witt Clinton, a member of a well-known family, was born on March 2, 1769 in Little Britain, New York. His father was a general who fought in the American Revolution. For his ninth birthday De Witt received a uniform that was exactly the same as an American soldier's uniform.

De Witt graduated from college and then studied to be a lawyer. He worked for his uncle, George Clinton, who was then **governor** of New York State. By 1798 De Witt had decided to be a politician. He served in the New York State legislature and as a United States Senator from New York. He was also **mayor** of New York City and governor of New York State. In 1812 Clinton ran for President, but he lost to James Madison.

De Witt Clinton headed a board to build the Erie Canal, which would connect the Hudson River with Lake Erie. Those who opposed the plan called it "Clinton's Folly," and "The Big Ditch." But Clinton worked to make the plan come true.

In October, 1825, it was Clinton's job as New York governor to open the 363-mile-long canal. He traveled on the first voyage from Lake Erie to the Atlantic Ocean. The new canal opened an important route for settlers and **immigrants** to reach the new states being carved out of the Northwest Territory.

About Clinton County

Land and resources: The land in Clinton County is somewhat hilly in the northern section and level in the southern part. Over 90 percent of the land is used for farming, but there are also some forests of hardwoods. The county has deposits of limestone, dolomite, sand, gravel, and shale.

People and their work: Farmers in the county raise many hogs and pigs. They also grow crops such as soybeans, corn, winter wheat, and oats. About 35 percent of the county's people work in factories. One of these factories, in Frankfort, makes Almond Joy, Power House, and Mounds candy bars. Other people in Clinton County have jobs in stores or are professional workers such as lawyers, doctors, or teachers.

Facts to remember about Clinton County: Michigantown, located along the Michigan Road, was an important stop for stagecoaches in the 1800s. In the mid-1900s, Clinton County was an important railroad center.

Crawford County

Named for: William Crawford
Date organized: 1818

William Crawford was born in Virginia in 1732. When he grew up, he became both a farmer and a surveyor. He met George Washington* and the two became friends. Just as Washington did, Crawford joined in the wars and battles that took place in America at that time. Crawford fought in the **French and Indian War** and took part in other battles against the Indians.

Ten years before the American Revolution began, Crawford moved to western Pennsylvania with his family. Here he became a **land agent** for George Washington. But with the outbreak of the Revolution, Crawford went back to a military career. As a lieutenant colonel of a Virginia unit of soldiers, he fought in some of the major battles in the early years of the Revolution.

As the war wore on, Crawford was assigned to the frontier, where he was to fight Indians who were **allies** of the British. He and his men built forts on the Allegheny River and the Ohio River. Then he resigned from the army.

Crawford's life of peace did not last. He was called back in 1782 to fight Indians living along the Sandusky River in what is now northern Ohio. His army was a poor one, and one of the better soldiers later wrote that they were nothing but a "party of clodhoppers." The Indians along the Sandusky were especially angry at Americans because of a terrible attack that had been made upon a peaceful and unarmed group of **Moravian Indians**. Some of the soldiers in Crawford's army had taken part in that disgraceful battle.

When Crawford and his men finally reached the Indian village, they were surrounded by Indians. Some of the soldiers retreated, and Crawford and an army doctor were captured. Crawford was tortured and finally killed by the angry Indians who were friends and relatives of the Moravians. The doctor was able to escape and bring back the news of Crawford's death.

No doubt people of the time thought of Crawford as a hero who suffered unfairly. He was, in fact, caught in a circle of unfairness. Indians struck out, often cruelly, at settlers who invaded their land. Settlers repaid the Indians by other cruel acts, and then the Indian people again struck back. It was a circle that took the lives of many good people, both white and Indian.

* See Washington County.

About Crawford County

<u>Land and resources:</u> Crawford County is hilly, and forests cover much of the land. The Ohio River runs along the county's southeastern border. There are thirty-one known caves in the county. One of the state's most beautiful rivers, the Blue, winds

its way through the county. Other resources include oil and gas, sandstone, limestone, and shale.

<u>People and their work:</u> Crawford has fewer people than most Indiana counties. Many of them work in other counties. Others have jobs in food stores and restaurants, and some are farmers who raise cattle or chickens. The main crops in the county are corn and oats.

<u>Facts to remember about Crawford County:</u> Spelunkers, or people who like to explore caves, love Crawford County. One of the county's caves, Wyandotte Cave, is world famous. In one of the cave's large rooms is a hill which is 135 feet tall! Wyandotte Cave also has the largest cave rooms in the world. If you were to walk around the outside of this room, you would walk about a half mile! In this room is one of the world's largest **stalagmites.**

Wyandotte Cave

Daviess County

Named for: Joseph Hamilton Daviess

Date organized: 1817

Born in Virginia on March 4, 1774, Joseph Hamilton Daviess moved with his family to Kentucky when he was five. He had no schooling until he was twelve, but like other boys who lived in the wilderness, he was skilled in handling guns. At the age of eighteen he took part in battles against Indians in the Northwest Territory.

Even though Joseph had only a few years of schooling as a boy, he began to study law and eventually started a practice in Danville, Kentucky. When John Adams was President, he named Joseph **district attorney** for Kentucky. During this time Joseph argued a case before the Supreme Court of the United States. At first other lawyers made fun of the backwoods lawyer from Kentucky. But Joseph soon gained their respect. Even Chief Justice John Marshall* was impressed, and Joseph later married Marshall's sister, Ann.

After serving as district attorney, Joseph Daviess moved to Lexington, Kentucky, and continued to practice law. He also became a volunteer in the Kentucky **militia**. As a major, he commanded several troops. In 1811 he and his men set out to join

41

William Henry Harrison,** who was ordered to stop a rebellion of Indians near what is now Lafayette, Indiana.

Daviess and his men met the Indiana soldiers at a new fort along the Wabash River. It was named Fort Harrison, and Daviess gave a speech dedicating it to William Henry Harrison, who was already a hero. A few days later the combined army marched north into battle. Daviess was killed while leading his men in a charge at the famous Battle of Tippecanoe.***

See Marshall County.
**See Harrison County.*
***See Tippecanoe County.*

About Daviess County

Land and resources: Most of the western and central part of the county is level, while the eastern and southern parts are hilly. The forests in the county are made up largely of oak and hickory trees. Coal is mined in the county, and the area also has oil, natural gas, sand, and gravel resources.

People and their work: Farmers in Daviess County raise cows, poultry, and hogs. They also grow such crops as corn, winter wheat, and hay. Other people in the county work in factories, automobile repair shops, and in the county's coal mines.

Facts to remember about Daviess County: Washington, the county seat, was an important stop along one of the state's early roads, the Vincennes and New Albany Turnpike. Travelers had to pay to use this macadam, or road made of broken stone and tar. Today Daviess County is known for raising turkeys.

Dearborn County

Named for: Henry Dearborn
Date organized: 1803

Henry Dearborn was born in Hampton, New Hampshire, on February 23, 1751. When he finished school, he set up a medical practice. He was not a doctor for long, however. When the Revolutionary War began, Dearborn gave up his practice and organized a militia in which he served as captain.

During the Revolutionary War, Dearborn took part in such famous battles as **Bunker Hill** and **Yorktown**. He served with General George Washington* at **Valley Forge**. He was also taken as a prisoner of war by the British, but was later released.

Dearborn's military career turned into a political one after the Revolutionary War. George Washington appointed him United States **marshall** for the district of Maine. In 1792 Dearborn was elected to Congress, where he served two terms. When Thomas Jefferson** became President, Dearborn was named Secretary of War. In his job as Secretary, Dearborn ordered a fort built at the settlement of "Chikago." Because of the important role Fort Dearborn played in the history of Chicago, his name is still associated with the city. Dearborn was Secretary of War when Indiana citizens decided to name their county after him.

Dearborn continued to serve the nation for many years. He fought in the War of 1812 and also served as **minister** to Portugal under President James Monroe.* Henry Dearborn died in 1829.

About Dearborn County

Land and resources: The eastern part of the county lies in Kentucky Bluegrass country and has rolling hills with hardwood forests. The Whitewater River tumbles through the northeastern corner, while the Ohio River forms part of the county's eastern border. Plains make up much of the land in the remainder of the county.

People and their work: Nearly 80 percent of Dearborn County's people work in factories, a few which make liquor from special wells of water in the area. Many others travel to neighboring counties to work. (The county is close to the large city of Cincinnati, Ohio.) Farmers in the area raise cattle and grow crops such as corn and soybeans. Some also grow tobacco.

Facts to remember about Dearborn County: Dearborn was one of the first four Indiana counties to be formed and was once very much larger than it is today. Several counties were carved out of Dearborn, such as Switzerland, Franklin, and Wayne.

Decatur County

Named for: Stephen Decatur
Date organized: 1821

The son of a sailor, Stephen Decatur grew up in Maryland with the dream of becoming a seaman. Even though he was bothered by poor health and was encouraged by his mother to become a minister, Stephen was determined. With two of his friends he bought a boat and sailed it up and down the Delaware River, pretending to fight pirates. When he was old enough, he joined the United States Navy.

Stephen's life as a sailor was an exciting one. After five years in the Navy he became commander of the ship *Enterprise*. He undertook the daring job of entering pirate territory and burning a ship being held by pirates. In another battle with pirates, he and his men boarded a pirate ship and fought with them in hand-to-hand combat. Stephen was wounded, and his brother James was killed.

The War of 1812 took Stephen away from pirate duty for a time. He captured a British ship, but was later overrun by four British ships.

After the war Stephen Decatur returned to fighting pirates. He went to a famous pirate area, the Barbary Coast of northern

Africa. In his victories there he was able to get back many goods which had been stolen from U.S. ships. He also forced the pirates to promise not to attack U.S. ships again.

In 1815 Decatur was named **commissioner** of the Navy. Five years later, on March 22, 1820, he was killed in a **duel** with Commodore James Barron. But his daring life on the sea had made him a hero, even to people in an Indiana county far from the Atlantic coast.

About Decatur County

Land and resources: Much of Decatur County has rolling hills, except for the northwestern section which has more level land. The forests in the county are made up largely of hardwoods such as oak, hickory, beech, birch, and maple. People mine the sand and gravel deposits in the county. The area also has oil and gas, limestone, dolomite, and clay.

People and their work: Much of the county's land is in farms, and many of farmers here raise corn or hogs. Soybeans and winter wheat are also grown. Other county residents work in factories, stores, banks, and in health care services.

Facts to remember about Decatur County: Some of Indiana's earliest transportation routes crossed Decatur County. The Michigan Road ran from Michigan through South Bend, Indianapolis, and Greensburg to Madison on the Ohio River. The state's first railroad line also ran through Greensburg as it connected Madison on the Ohio River to Indianapolis. At first the railroad was made up of a single car drawn by horses.

DeKalb County

Named for: Baron Johann de Kalb
Date organized: 1837

The son of peasants named Kalb, Johann was born in Huttendorf, Germany. He had only a little education before going to work as a waiter. At the age of sixteen Johann left home and went to France. He added the title Baron to his name, feeling that it would make it possible for him to join the French army.

Kalb fought in several wars in Europe. While he served as a soldier, he also studied languages, math, and military planning. In 1767 Kalb traveled to the American colonies on a spy mission for the French. He was to test the colonists' feelings about the British. Kalb's mission was discovered by the British, and he was sent back to France.

Kalb returned to America when the French began to aid the colonies during the American Revolution. Kalb spent the first winter at Valley Forge with George Washington* and later fought in such famous battles as **Brandywine** and **Germantown**. Although he had come to America as a **soldier of fortune**, Kalb became a strong believer in the American cause.

In 1780 Kalb and his men were sent to Charleston, South Carolina, to aid General Horatio Gates. The American soldiers had little food and few supplies, and Kalb warned Gates not to attack the British army. But Gates did not listen. As he marched to a foolish attack, the British made their own surprise attack. Gates threw down his rifle and fled. Only Kalb and his men held their positions. Kalb did not give up and was said to have been wounded eleven times. He died a hero on August 19, 1780.

* See Washington County.

About DeKalb County

Land and resources: The land in DeKalb County is mostly level with a few hills along its northern and western borders. About 80 percent of it is used for farming. The county has deposits of oil and gas, peat, sand, and gravel. There are also hardwood forests, which include elm, oak, ash, cottonwood, and hickory trees.

People and their work: Milk is an important product of DeKalb County farms. Farmers also raise oats, hay, winter wheat, and corn. Almost half of the county's workers have jobs in factories. Others work in stores, while some have jobs dealing with recreation or amusements.

Facts to remember about DeKalb County: Automobile manufacturing was once important in Indiana. Auburn, the county's largest city, was the heart of this business, and over twenty-one models of cars were created there. Perhaps the most famous and expensive of these was the Duesenberg. Today a museum in Auburn houses many of these classic automobiles.

Delaware County

Named for: Delaware Indians
Date organized: 1827

The Delaware were a group of Indians who once lived in the area of the Delaware River and Delaware Bay in what is now the eastern United States. The Delaware called themselves the "Lenape" or "Lenni-Lenape." They were a powerful group who were respected by other Indian tribes in the region.

Generally the Delaware people had good relations with the Europeans who came to America, and they even made treaties with **William Penn**. But gradually the Delaware were pushed west by white settlers and by wars with their enemies, the **Iroquois Indians**.

In the 1700s the Delaware people settled in what is now eastern Ohio. They then moved on and established about fourteen villages between the present cities of Muncie and Indianapolis. Muncie, once called Muncie-town, was named for a **clan** of Delawares that once lived there.

One leader of the Delaware was Chief Anderson. His daughter, Mekinges, married a white fur trader named William Conner. They ran a trading post near what is now Noblesville. Conner and his brother were also scouts for Governor William Henry Harrison.*

The Delaware's villages in Indiana were not lasting. Several were destroyed when a military road was built through Delaware County. The arrival of white settlers forced many Indians from their land. In 1818 the Delaware gave up all their land in Indiana for a yearly payment of $4,000. Most moved to a reservation west of the Mississippi, including Mekinges and her six children.

* See Harrison County.

About Delaware County

<u>Land and resources:</u> Most of the land in Delaware County is level, with some hilly areas along the White and Mississinewa rivers. About three fourths of it is used for farming. There are some hardwood forests made up of oak, maple, beech, and birch trees. The county has deposits of sand and gravel, limestone, peat and **marl**.

<u>People and their work:</u> Many of the county's people are farmers who raise winter wheat, soybeans, oats, corn and tomatoes. Other people have professional jobs, such as teaching or practicing medicine or law. Many have jobs in offices, stores, or factories. One of these factories is the Ball Corporation, which is well-known for making home canning equipment.

<u>Facts to remember about Delaware County:</u> Muncie, the county seat, is the home of Ball State University, one of the state's largest universities. Ball State has a greenhouse with more types of **orchids** than any collection in the world.

Dubois County

Named for: Toussaint Dubois
Date organized: 1818

Dubois County was named for Toussaint Dubois, a French soldier and Indian trader. He was born in 1764 and lived in Vincennes, Indiana, where he ran a tavern and traded for furs with the Indians. When Vincennes became a town, Toussaint Dubois became one of the town's first **trustees**.

Touissant was married to Jeanne Bonneau, and the couple had six children. After Jeanne's death, he married Jane Baird. Her third son Jesse was a personal friend of Abraham Lincoln.

Dubois served as a spy, scout, and soldier for William Henry Harrison,* who was intent on destroying the Indians' power in the Indiana area. Dubois guided troops from Vincennes to a strong Indian village where the Indian leader called the **Prophet** was encouraging Indians to attack white settlers. Dubois carried messages from Harrison to Prophetstown. He also took part in the actual battle at Tippecanoe.**

Touissant Dubois died on March 1, 1816, when he was traveling from Kaskaskia to Vincennes. He drowned in the Little Wabash River, and his body was never found.

* See Harrison County.
** See Tippecanoe County.

About Dubois County

Land and resources: Most of the land in Dubois County is made up of hills and valleys. About 72 percent of it is used for farming. The hardwood forests in the county are made up largely of oak and hickory. The county's natural resources include deposits of oil and gas, clay, shale, sandstone, limestone, and coal. The Patoka River winds through the county as it makes its way west to join the Wabash.

People and their work: Dubois' farmers raise more poultry than farmers in other Indiana counties. A number of farmers also raise livestock and hay. Other people in the county are teachers, have jobs in offices and stores, or work in factories, many of which produce wood office furniture.

Facts to remember about Dubois County: The Buffalo Trace cuts through the northern part of the county. This trail was about 120 miles long and was once traveled by large herds of buffalo. Today a marker stands where the trail can still be seen.

Elkhart County

Named for: Elkhart River
Date organized: 1830

Elkhart County is named both for the Elkhart River and a band of Potawatomi Indians called the Elkhart Potawatomi. According to legends, the Miami Indians named the river Elkhart because of the many elk in the area. There is also an island near the river's mouth shaped like a heart. Thus, the two words were formed into one.

Early in the 1700s the Potawatomi Indians settled in the old Miami campgrounds. Their villages dotted the river banks, and they adopted the Miami name for the river. It was the Potawatomi who lived there when the first Europeans, the French, came. The French translated the Indian name into their own language, "Coeur-de-cerf," which means heart of a stag.

Although the Potawatomi were a peaceful people who used the river for trade and travel, they lost their land to white settlers. By 1840 land treaties were settled and the Potawatomi were forced to move to reservations west of the Mississippi River.

About Elkhart County

Land and resources: Most of the county has level land, with about 70 percent of it used for farming. The forests in the county are made up of hardwoods such as oak, hickory, maple, beech, and birch. There are also deposits of oil and gas, sand, gravel, and marl.

People and their work: Farmers in the county raise poultry and livestock and grow crops such as oats, corn, winter wheat, and soybeans. A large number of people work in the county's factories, which produce such items as musical instruments. A large factory in Middlebury makes motor homes, travel trailers, and custom vans.

Facts to remember about Elkhart County: Many of the state's Amish people live in Elkhart County. Tourists visit Nappanee and Middlebury to enjoy the good foods and buy Amish crafts. Goshen College is located in Goshen, the county seat.

Fayette County

Named for: Marquis de Lafayette
Date organized: 1819

Marie-Joseph-Paul-Yves-Roch-Gilbert du Motier, Marquis de Lafayette, was born to an important French family in 1757. By the age of sixteen he was already a soldier and had also married. He was excited by the Americans' fight for freedom from Great Britain and in 1776 went to America to become a soldier there.

Americans were unsure of Lafayette's desire to be part of the Revolution. But Lafayette asked only two favors: not to be paid and to work with George Washington!* Soon Washington and Lafayette became close friends.

Lafayette proved his ability and became a leader of American troops. He suffered with Washington and his men during the winter at Valley Forge. For a time, Lafayette returned home and tried to convince the French government to help the Americans. He then went back to America and continued to help the colonists win the war.

After the American Revolution, Lafayette returned to France, where he hoped to become the George Washington of his people. Although he was popular among the common people and had an important part in the **French Revolution**, he also suffered for his political views and spent time in prison.

From July, 1824, to September, 1825, Lafayette visited the United States and was greeted by record crowds of people. During his stay he traveled to Indiana. A feast was held in his honor at Jeffersonville. The state militia was present at the feast and children spread flowers on his path as he walked to the table. There was a great arch with the words, "Indiana welcomes Lafayette, the Champion of liberty in both hemispheres."

A great hero in two nations, Lafayette returned to France and continued his work in the government there. He died in Paris, France, on May 20, 1834.

See Washington County.

About Fayette County

Land and resources: Fayette County has level land and areas of hilly land. About 80 percent of it is used for farming. There are hardwood forests that include such trees as oak and hickory. The county has deposits of oil and gas as well as sand and gravel. The Whitewater River cuts through the center of the county.

People and their work: Many farmers in the county raise hogs and grow crops such as soybeans and corn. Other people have jobs in factories or in businesses such as auto repair shops or health services.

Facts to remember about Fayette County: The Whitewater Canal once cut through the county, connecting the National Road with the Ohio River. Connersville, the county seat, was the home of eight different makes of automobiles in the early 1900s.

Above is an old drawing of John Chapman, better known as Johnny Appleseed. This pioneer who lived in the Ohio-Indiana region planted apple trees and gave out appleseeds to farmers wherever he went. Chapman died and is buried in Allen County.

The other photos on this page show Daniel Boone (upper right) and Lewis Cass. Two Indiana counties are named after these men. The stories of their lives appear on pages 19 and 26.

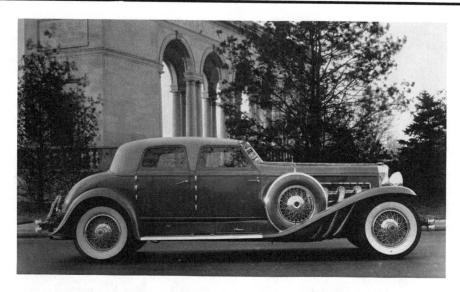

The costly and speedy Duesenberg automobile (above) was produced in Auburn (DeKalb County) in the 1920s -1930s. Below are the well-known canning jars which made the Ball Corporation in Muncie (Delaware County) famous.

Floyd County

Named for: John Floyd and/or
Davis Floyd
Date organized: 1819

John Floyd was born in Virginia in 1751. Following in the footsteps of his father, John became a surveyor and worked in the Ohio Valley, buying some of the land for himself. He traveled into the Kentucky area, where he became friends with George Rogers Clark* and Daniel Boone.** Floyd helped rescue Boone's daughter, Jemima, who was captured by Indians.

When the Revolutionary War began, John Floyd enlisted in the colonial navy. His ship was captured by the British, and John was taken to England, where he was put in prison. Eventually he managed to escape and return to America.

After the Revolutionary War, John Floyd and several other Floyd families moved to Kentucky and formed a settlement called Floyd's Station. Indian attacks on the settlement were common, however, and on one occasion John was severely wounded. He died shortly afterward in the year 1783.

Although many sources say that Floyd County is named for John Floyd, it is also possible the county was named for Davis Floyd. Davis Floyd was a lawyer who contributed to the growth of Floyd County. In addition to his law practice, he ran a tavern and operated a ferry on the Ohio River. Davis Floyd also held political offices. He served as a judge, a member of the Territorial Legislature, and the Indiana General Assembly. He was one of the most popular men in the Indiana Territory, and a village in the county, Floyd Knobs, is named in his honor.

* See Clark County.
** See Boone County.

About Floyd County

<u>Land and resources:</u> The Ohio River flows along the southeastern boundary of Floyd County. Much of the land is hilly and covered with forests of oak and hickory. The county also has natural resources of sand and gravel as well as oil and gas.

<u>People and their work:</u> A large number of the county's people go to neighboring counties to work. Others have jobs in factories, some that produce wood products such as plywood and furniture. Farmers in the county raise mushrooms, hay, oats, and other crops.

<u>Facts to remember about Floyd County:</u> Steamboat building was an important part of the county's past. One of the most famous steamers on the Ohio and Mississippi rivers, the *Robert E. Lee,* was built at New Albany, the county seat. In 1853 citizens of New Albany opened the first public high school in Indiana.

Fountain County

Named for: James Fontaine
Date organized: 1825

Little is known about the life of James Fontaine, except that he was an Army officer from Kentucky. After the Americans defeated the British in the Revolutionary War, the new American government opened the land north and west of the Ohio River to settlers. Indians who lived in this area, called the Northwest Territory, were angry about the takeover of their land and often attacked the new settlers. Major James Fontaine fought under the command of General Josiah Harmer to try to defeat the Indians.

General Harmer's strikes against the Indians began in the fall of 1790, with Major Fontaine in charge of some of the soldiers. The army traveled north from Fort Washington in Cincinnati with orders to destroy all Indian towns between the Ohio River and what is today Fort Wayne. They were also ordered to destroy Indian crops of corn and vegetables.

When Harmer reached his destination near the Fort Wayne site, he found the Indian villages deserted. The soldiers set fire to the houses and cornfields. Three separate columns of troops were sent out to find the Indians in the forests.

On October 22, 1790, Harmer's troops were badly defeated by the Indians in what came to be known as the Battle of the Maumee. Among the officers killed was James Fontaine. He was buried in a trench near the banks of the Maumee River. Peace with the Indians in the area was not reached until 1794 with the victories of General Anthony Wayne.*

* *See Wayne County.*

About Fountain County

Land and resources: Most of the county has level land with about 84 percent of it used for farming. There are some hardwood forests made up largely of oak and hickory. The county has mineral deposits of sand and gravel, oil and gas, clay, and coal. The Wabash River forms the county's western border.

People and their work: Many of the county's people are farmers who grow corn and soybeans. Others work in factories, have jobs in stores and businesses, or are professional workers such as doctors and teachers.

Facts to remember about Fountain County: In the northwestern part of the county is Portland Arch, a large natural bridge made of sandstone. The county was the home of Daniel W. Voorhees, who represented Indiana for many years in the U. S. Congress.

Franklin County

Named for: Benjamin Franklin
Date organized: 1811

One of seventeen children, Benjamin Franklin was born in Boston, Massachusetts, on January 17, 1706. Young Ben had less than two years of schooling, but his mind was always busy learning. As a teenager, he was an **apprentice** in his brother's printing shop. There he learned many skills, including writing and producing a newspaper.

When Ben was seventeen, he quarreled with his brother and ran away to Philadelphia. Within a few years, Ben was printing his own newspaper, the *Pennsylvania Gazette*. Soon he became a wealthy man with his printing, publishing, and writing. One of his publications was *Poor Richard's Almanac*. This yearly publication contained many facts and also had jokes and **proverbs** that people still quote today.

By the time he was thirty, Ben began a life of public service. He served in the Pennsylvania legislature and started the first library in the colonies. He also became Philadelphia's **postmaster** and set up street cleaning and fire departments as well.

With all his jobs, Ben Franklin continued studying. He taught himself to read several languages and play several musical instruments. He was interested in science and became one of the greatest scientists and inventors of his time. He is especially remembered for his part in the discovery of electricity. His other inventions included the lightning rod, **bifocal glasses,** and an iron stove and chimney that produced more heat than a fireplace.

Ben Franklin spent many years in Europe trying to improve relations between England and the colonies. Later he tried to convince France to support the Americans' fight for freedom. He was the only man to sign four of the most important documents in the founding of the United States: the Declaration of Independence, the **Treaty of Alliance** with France, the Constitution, and the **Treaty of Paris**. Benjamin Franklin died on April 17, 1790.

About Franklin County

<u>Land and resources:</u> The land in northeastern Franklin County is mostly level, while rolling hills cover the rest of the county. The county has hardwood forests that include oak, hickory, maple, beech, and birch. It also has deposits sand and gravel, oil and gas, as well as limestone. The Whitewater River flows through the county on its journey to join the Ohio.

<u>People and their work:</u> Farmers in Franklin County raise livestock and crops such as tobacco. Many other people work in factories or drive to jobs in nearby counties.

<u>Facts to remember about Franklin County:</u> Part of the Whitewater Canal that was built in the 1800s has been restored in the county in the small town of Metamora. Visitors come to ride in a canal boat that was once a common sight in the region.

Fulton County

Named for: Robert Fulton
Date organized: 1836

Robert Fulton was born on November 14, 1765, in Lancaster County, Pennsylvania. The son of poor Irish parents, Robert became an **apprentice** in the jewelry trade. But Robert was more interested in art and spent much time painting. He earned enough money painting portraits to travel to London, England. There he studied under the famous **Benjamin West**.

While in England, Fulton met an engineer interested in canal building. Fulton became interested in canal systems and in boats. He worked in France for nine years designing and building a submarine called the *Nautilus*. The ship was too far ahead of its time, however, and was considered useless.

Fulton turned his attention to making workable steamboats. The first one sank on the Seine River in France, but Fulton was determined. With the encouragement and money of Robert Livingston, an American minister in France, Fulton returned to the United States. There he began building the *Clermont*, which people at first called Fulton's Folly.

On August 17, 1806, the *Clermont* proved its worth, steaming up the Hudson River from New York to Albany at the rate of five miles per hour. Although other steamboats had been

65

built, Fulton's was practical for carrying both freight and passengers. Fulton and Livingston were granted the right to run their steamboats in New York for thirty years. Fulton was also asked to build steamships for the United States government for military purposes. The first one was named the *Fulton*.

About Fulton County

Land and resources: The land in Fulton County is level with nearly 80 percent of it used for farming. There are some forests of oak and hickory. The county has deposits of sand and gravel, oil and gas, peat, and marl. The Tippecanoe River flows through the northern part of the county.

People and their work: Farmers in the county grow corn, soybeans, oats, and hay. They also raise hogs and dairy cows. Other people work in factories or have jobs in businesses such as insurance or health agencies.

Facts to remember about Fulton County: The county had many round barns, which were built around 1900. Their popularity did not last and only a few still remain.

Gibson County

Named for: John Gibson
Date organized: 1813

John Gibson was born May 23, 1740, in Lancaster, Pennsylvania. He spent his first fifty years as a soldier, an Indian fighter, a frontiersman, scout, fur trader, and Indian **interpreter** in the area of Pittsburgh, Pennsylvania. In 1763 he was captured by Indians. Luckily, an Indian woman rushed in and saved him from death. They were later married. The Indians grew to like John. They nicknamed him Horse-head, which meant he had horse sense, or common sense.

When the American Revolution began, Gibson became a captain in the American army and served with George Washington* at Valley Forge. The following year he commanded a small, isolated fort surrounded by thousands of Indians who were fighting for the British. Supplies were few and fuel was short. The men became so hungry they ate roots and their rawhide clothing. By summer, only half of Gibson's men were still alive.

After John and his men were rescued by American soldiers, John was made commander in chief of the western frontier. At the age of sixty he was named Secretary of the Indiana Territory by Thomas Jefferson.** Gibson held that post for sixteen years, until Indiana became a state. In his later years Gibson returned to Pennsylvania to live with his son-in-law. He died there in 1822.

See Washington County.
**See Jefferson County.*

About Gibson County

Land and resources: Much of the land in Gibson County is hilly, except in the central area. There is also more level land in the western section, where the White River and Patoka River meet the Wabash. Many of the hills have forests of hickory and oak. The county also has deposits of oil and gas, sand and gravel, clay, coal, and limestone.

People and their work: Farmers in Gibson County raise many types of crops, but the most important one is winter wheat. Other people have jobs as teachers or jobs in health care. Some people work in the county's factories and coal mines.

Facts to remember about Gibson County: Fort Branch was built in Gibson County by General William Henry Harrison in 1811 to protect the region from Indian attack.

Grant County

Named for: Samuel and Moses
Grant
Date organized: 1831

Not very much is known about the brothers, Samuel and Moses Grant. Samuel was born November 29, 1762. He was a surveyor in Lincoln County, Kentucky, in 1781. He also served as a captain in a Kentucky militia. Samuel married Lydia Craig, and the couple had two children. Moses Grant was born October 3, 1768, but there seems to be no recorded history of his life. He died at an early age and was unmarried.

We do know something about the deaths of Samuel and Moses Grant, however. In August of 1789 a large group of Indians camped on the north side of the Ohio River. Records state that the Indians often crossed the river and "did a good deal of mischief." A company of soldiers, including Moses and Samuel, crossed the river to drive them away.

A battle took place between the Indians and soldiers near a stream in what is now Switzerland County,* Indiana. Samuel Grant was hiding behind a tree and taking aim at an Indian when he was fatally shot by a second Indian. Moses ran to the aid of

69

his brother, but he too was shot and killed. The stream where the battle took place has since been called Grants' Creek.

See Switzerland County.

About Grant County

Land and resources: The land in Grant county is mostly level with some rolling areas in the central and eastern sections. Much of the land is used for farming, and there are hardwood forests that include oak, hickory, maple, beech, and birch. The county has deposits of sand and gravel, peat, and limestone. The Mississinewa River flows through the center of the county.

People and their work: Farmers in the county raise soybeans, winter wheat, corn, oats, and tomatoes. A number of the county's people are doctors, lawyers, and teachers. Others work in factories that produce such items as glass and paper products, automobile parts, and video parts.

Facts to remember about Grant County: The county was an important oil and gas producing area in the early 1900s. James Dean, a movie hero of the 1950s, grew up in the town of Fairmount in the southern part of the county and is buried here.

Greene County

Named for: Nathaniel Greene
Date organized: 1821

Nathaniel Greene was born to a Quaker family in Rhode Island on August 7, 1742. People of the Quaker faith did not believe in any type of fighting. But Nathaniel believed that the colonists should resist the King of England even if it took force. He also attended a military parade. For these reasons the Quakers no longer felt he was one of them, and he was dismissed from his church.

At the age of twenty-eight, Greene joined the Rhode Island militia. He quickly rose from the rank of private to that of major general. In 1775 he led the Rhode Island troops that were sent to become part of the Continental, or American, army.

One of Greene's jobs in the Continental army was to find supplies. It was not easy to find food and clothing for the soldiers, especially during the hard winter at Valley Forge. Greene was so devoted to his work he even sold his own land to raise money so that the soldiers could have the food and equipment they needed.

Greene also led troops in battle. In the fall of 1780 he was made head of the southern army, which had nearly been wiped out by the British. Greene broke the army down into smaller bands. (One of these bands was led by Francis Marion.*) These small groups worked much like Indian forces and drove the British out of one fort after another. By doing this Greene and his men gained control of South Carolina and Georgia.

When the American Revolution ended, Greene was rewarded for his services. The grateful governments of South Carolina and Georgia gave him both money and land. Greene lived on a plantation in Georgia until his death in 1786.

See Marion County.

About Greene County

Land and resources: Most of Greene County is hilly except for the central area, which has more level land. Many types of trees grow in the county's hardwood forests. They include oak, hickory, ash, honeylocust, maple, and black walnut. The county has deposits of oil and gas, sand and gravel, clay, shale, and limestone. The Eel and White rivers flow through the county. There are also nine caves in the area.

People and their work: A little more than half the land in the county is used for farming, and farmers raise cattle and crops such as corn, soybeans, and hay. Many of the county's people work in stores, banks, and factories. Others go to work outside Greene County.

Facts to remember about Greene County: The county has one of the largest viaducts, or railroad bridges, in the world. It was built in 1906 by the Illinois Central Railroad.

Hamilton County

Named for: Alexander Hamilton
Date organized: 1823

Alexander Hamilton, who became U.S. Secretary of the Treasury, was born January 11, 1757, on Nevis Island in the **West Indies**. When he was twelve, his father lost all his wealth and Alexander was sent to work at a counting house, or a place that keeps track of a business's money. The boy showed unusual talent and intelligence in his work.

When his mother died Alexander was sent to New Jersey to live with relatives. In America he attended several schools. At the outbreak of the American Revolution, Hamilton sided with the colonists. He gave speeches and wrote pamphlets and newspaper articles. He was also selected to be George Washington's* private secretary and aide. He and Washington formed a friendship that was to last a lifetime.

After the Revolution, Hamilton helped shape the new government. George Washington appointed him Secretary of the Treasury. Hamilton's talent for working with money helped build a solid foundation for our government's financial system. He became unpopular with the other founding fathers, however, since he did not truly believe in democracy. He wanted a strong central government modeled after England.

Unfortunately, Alexander Hamilton's life was cut short in a senseless and tragic way. He disagreed publically with Aaron Burr, who had been Vice President. As a result, Burr lost an important election and challenged Hamilton to a duel. Although Hamilton accepted the challenge, he refused to fire his pistol. Burr shot Hamilton, who died the following day, July 12, 1804.

* See Washington County.

About Hamilton County

Land and resources: Most of Hamilton County is made up of level land, with over 65 percent of it used for farming. The county has hardwood forests that include oak, hickory, maple, birch, and beech. It also has deposits of sand and gravel as well as peat. Its water resources include the west fork of the White River and the Morse Reservoir.

People and their work: Many of Hamilton County's farmers raise hogs and grow crops such as corn and soybeans. Other people work in factories, stores, and businesses such as insurance and banks. A large number of people have jobs in neighboring counties.

Facts to remember about Hamilton County: Indiana's past is recreated at Conner Prairie Pioneer Settlement near Noblesville. Houses, shops, a school, and other buildings have been rebuilt as they were in 1836.

Hancock County

Named for: John Hancock
Date organized: 1828

John Hancock was born January 23, 1737, in Braintree, Massachusetts. His father died when he was only seven, and John was sent to live with a wealthy uncle. There he was well educated by private teachers and in Boston grammar schools. He was sent to Harvard College at the age of thirteen.

After college John began working with his uncle as a shipping merchant. When his uncle died, the business was left to John. He became one of the wealthiest men in New England.

John took an active role in helping the colonists earn their freedom from Great Britain. He also used much of his money to help the cause. The British considered Hancock an outlaw, because, being opposed to British taxes, he refused to do business with them. He had to flee Boston so that he would not be arrested.

John traveled to Philadelphia, where he was active in helping form our nation's government. He served as president of the Second Continental Congress from 1775 to 1777. When the Declaration of Independence was completed, he signed it in large, bold letters. He said, "I write so that George III may read without his spectacles." Today people often say they are writing their "John Hancock" when they sign a paper or document.

John Hancock held several other public offices. He commanded the Massachusetts militia and helped write the constitution for the state of Massachusetts. He also served as its governor from 1780 to 1785 and again from 1787 to 1793. He died in Quincy, Massachusetts, at the age of fifty-six.

* See Washington County.

About Hancock County

Land and resources: Most of Hancock County has level land with over 80 percent of it used for farming. There are hardwood forests of maple, birch, and beech, and the county also has deposits of sand and gravel, oil and gas, as well as peat. The Big Blue River cuts through the southeastern corner of the county.

People and their work: Hancock's farmers raise hogs and grow corn and soybeans. Many of the county's people have jobs outside the county in the city of Indianapolis. Others work in stores and factories in the county.

Facts to remember about Hancock County: James Whitcomb Riley, a famous poet, grew up in Greenfield. He is remembered for poems such as "Little Orphan Annie" and "The Old Swimmin' Hole."

Harrison County

Named for: William Henry
Harrison
Date organized: 1808

William Henry Harrison, known as "the father of Indiana," was born in Charles City County, Virginia, on February 9, 1773. His father Benjamin Harrison was a signer of the Declaration of Independence. As a boy, William would rather hunt and fish than read and study. Still, he graduated from a college in Virginia and then studied medicine under Dr. Benjamin Rush* in Philadelphia.

When he was eighteen, William left his study of medicine to join the United States army. He served in the Northwest Territory as the army tried to keep Indians from attacking settlers. William served as an aide to General Anthony Wayne* and fought with him at the **Battle of the Fallen Timbers**.

Harrison became involved in politics in the Northwest Territory. In 1798 he was appointed secretary of the Northwest Territory which included Indiana. From 1801 to 1812 he was governor of the Indiana Territory. During that time boundaries changed, and the Indiana Territory included parts of the present states of Indiana, Michigan, Illinois, Wisconsin, and Minnesota.

While Harrison was governor of the Indiana Territory, two Indian leaders, Tecumseh and his brother who was called the

Prophet, tried to unite Indians to fight the white settlers moving into this region. Harrison organized an army of about 1,000 men and marched to Tecumseh's village located where the Tippecanoe empties into the Wabash River. Tecumseh was away and had ordered his brother to keep the peace until all Indians were united. But on November 7, 1811, the Prophet led an attack against Harrison's army. The Indians were defeated and their villages destroyed. Because it was called the Battle of Tippecanoe,** Harrison earned the nickname, Old Tippecanoe.

After the Battle of Tippecanoe Harrison held several offices, including United States Senator from Ohio. Nearly thirty years after the Battle of Tippecanoe, he ran for President of the United States with John Tyler as his Vice President. Their campaign saying was "Tippecanoe and Tyler too." Harrison was elected the ninth President of the United States. One month after he took office in 1841, however, he died of pneumonia. One of the grandsons of William and Anna Symmes Harrison later became the 23rd President of the United States. He was Benjamin Harrison.

*See Wayne County.
**See Tippecanoe County.

About Harrison County

Land and resources: Much of the land in Harrison County is hilly. There are many hardwood forests which include oak and hickory trees. The county has deposits of sand and gravel, oil and gas, as well as limestone. The Ohio River makes up the county's southern border and the Blue River runs along much of its eastern edge. There are 76 caves in the county, more than in any county in the United States.

People and their work: Farmers in the county raise cattle and grow crops such as tobacco and winter wheat. About half of the county's workers go to jobs outside the county. Others stay in Harrison and work in factories, stores, and banks.

Facts to remember about Harrison County: Although Corydon is a small town today that serves as the county seat, it was Indiana's first capital. South of Corydon is a formation of caves known as Squire Boone Caverns. The caves are named after Daniel Boone's older brother who lived nearby. The caves have streams, waterfalls, stalactites, and stalagmites.

This building at Corydon served as the state capitol from 1816 to 1825. Today it is a museum.

Hoosiers named their counties after important leaders such as the ones shown above. Left to right are Benjamin Franklin, Thomas Jefferson, Alexander Hamilton, and George Washington.

Hendricks County

Named for: William Hendricks
Date organized: 1824

William Hendricks, a political leader in Indiana, was born in Pennsylvania in 1783. William received a good education and graduated from Jefferson College in 1810. He traveled west to Cincinnati, studied law, and became a lawyer in 1812. Then he moved to Madison, Indiana where he lived for the rest of his life, marrying a woman named Ann Paul.

In Indiana William's career changed to politics and public service. He served as one of Indiana's members to the United States House of Representatives from 1816 to 1822. He then became governor of the state.

While Hendricks was governor the state capital was moved from Corydon to Indianapolis. Hendricks County was also established and named for him. Shortly before Hendricks' job as governor ended, he was elected as a United States Senator from Indiana.

William Hendricks worked hard to build roads and canals in the state. He also felt the state should have a good system of education, and he supported the work of building Hanover College and Indiana State University at Bloomington.

About Hendricks County

<u>Land and resources:</u> Hendricks County has both areas of level land and rolling hills. It has hardwood forests of oak and hickory as well as deposits of sand, gravel and shale. The Big Walnut Creek cuts through the northwest corner of the county.

<u>People and their work:</u> Farmers in Hendricks County raise livestock and grow such crops as corn and soybeans. A large number of the county's people go to other counties to work. Others stay in Hendricks and work in factories, stores, and at a large **utility company** that provides electric power to the region.

<u>Facts to remember about Hendricks County:</u> The National Road which led thousands of settlers westward, ran through the southern section of the county. A movie star, Forrest Tucker, went to school in Plainfield.

Henry County

Named for: Patrick Henry
Date organized: 1822

Patrick Henry, governor of Virginia, was born May 29, 1736. Patrick was not thought of as a good student in the country school he attended. He showed more skill at hunting, fishing, and playing the fiddle. He also failed in several careers as a young man. Although he was interested in keeping a store, he and his brother failed as merchants. Patrick also found he was unable to make a living as a farmer.

Patrick Henry finally found he was both interested and skilled at law. He studied law and became a lawyer at the age of 24. He was popular with frontier farmers and was also a good speaker.

Henry's background of law and speaking led him into politics. He was member of the government in the Virigina colony. He then served the colonies in the first Continental Congress. He tried to convince other lawmakers to prepare for war with Great Britain. In a famous speech he said, "I know not what course others may take, but as for me, give me liberty or give me death."

From 1776 to 1778 and again from 1784 to 1786 Henry was governor of Virginia. During his first term he sent George

Rogers Clark* to capture the British forts in the area of Indiana and Illinois. Patrick Henry died on June 6, 1799.

*See Clark County.

About Henry County

<u>Land and resources:</u> Most of Henry County has level land with over 75 percent of it used for farming. It has hardwood forests made up of maple, beech, and birch trees. The county has deposits of sand and gravel as well as peat. The Big Blue River flows through the county.

<u>People and their work:</u> Farmers in the county raise livestock and grow crops such as soybeans and corn. Other people work in factories that make products such as automobile parts and many steel items. Some people have jobs in recreation areas or in hospitals and other health care businesses. Still others go outside the county to work.

<u>Facts to remember about Henry County:</u> The county is the birthplace of Wilbur Wright. With his brother, Orville, Wilbur built the first successful airplane in 1903.

Howard County

Named for: Tilghaman A. Howard
Date organized: 1844

Howard County was first known as Richardville County. Its first name honored Jean Baptiste Richardville, a chief of the Miami Indians. Richardville, whose Indian name was Pe-che-wa, worked for peace between the Indians and settlers. He also became wealthy by controlling the fur trade in the area.

Two years after it was organized, Richardville County's name was changed to Howard County. This was done to honor Tilghaman A. Howard, a man who served his state as a lawyer and lawmaker.

Tilghaman was born near Pickensville, South Carolina, on November 14, 1797. He went to a public school as a boy and later studied law. He began his law practice in Knoxville, Tennessee. In 1824 he also served as a lawmaker in the Tennessee state government.

Howard moved to Indiana and practiced law in Bloomington and Rockville. He served as a representative from Indiana in the United States House of Representatives. Later he was sent by the United States government to help direct affairs in Texas before it became a state. Howard died in Texas in 1844.

About Howard County

Land and resources: Most of the land in Howard County is level, and about 80 percent of it is used for farming. There are some hardwood forests in the county which are made up of oak, hickory, elm, ash, and cottonwood. The county also has deposits of sand and gravel, clay, shale, limestone, and peat.

People and their work: Farmers in the county raise corn, soybeans, and winter wheat. Other people work in schools, stores, and offices. Many work in factories that make products such as automobile parts.

Facts to remember about Howard County: Kokomo, Howard County's county seat, is called the "City of Firsts." An inventor named Elwood Haynes created stainless steel dinnerware, an automobile, and other inventions. The first canned tomato juice, the first mechanical corn picker, and the first rubber tire pumped full of air also came from Kokomo.

Elwood Haynes built an automobile in 1894. The car could travel seven miles an hour.

Huntington County

Named for: Samuel Huntington
Date organized: 1834

Samuel Huntington, a signer of the Declaration of Independence, was born in Windham, Connecticut, on July 3, 1731. Samuel grew up on a farm and had little schooling. But he loved to read books and learned on his own from them. At age sixteen Samuel became an apprentice to a cooper, or barrel maker. But he wanted to learn more than the skill of a cooper and began to study law on his own.

Huntington, a self-made lawyer earned his license to practice law at the age of 27 and set up practice. People who lived and worked with Huntington liked him and admired him for his hard work. He was appointed to many committees and elected to public offices. For nearly ten years he represented Connecticut in the Continental Congress. He was also president of that group for two years.

In 1786 Huntington was elected governor of Connecticut. He was reelected to that job each year for ten years. Samuel Huntington died on January 5, 1796, at the age of 64.

About Huntington County

Land and resources: Huntington County is made up of level and slightly rolling land. It has hardwood forests that include oak, hickory, maple, beech, and white ash trees. It also has deposits of sand and gravel, shale, clay, limestone, and dolomite. The Wabash River and the Salamonie River both make their way through the county. People from all over the state visit the county to enjoy water sports and other activities at Huntington Lake and Salamonie Reservoir.

People and their work: Much of the land in Huntington County is used for farming, and farmers grow crops such as soybeans, corn, oats, and hay. They also raise pigs and cattle. Other people in the county work in schools, factories, and stores.

Facts to remember about Huntington County: The county seat of Huntington was once called Wepecheange, meaning place of "flints." (Indians used a special stone called flint to make arrowheads and knives.) Miami Indians once lived in the Huntington area.

Jackson County

Named for: Andrew Jackson
Date organized: 1816

Andrew Jackson was born on March 15, 1767, in Waxhaw, South Carolina. His father died just before Andrew was born, so he and his mother and two brothers lived with his uncle. Andrew attended school a total of one year. He was absent because of measles, mumps, chicken pox, a broken leg from a fall off a horse and one from a fall from a grapevine.

Andrew's boyhood was also affected by the Revolutionary War. One of his brothers was killed in battle. When Andrew was thirteen, he and his other brother, Robert, joined the colonists' cause and delivered messages for them. Eventually the boys were captured by the British. When Andrew refused to polish the boots of a British officer, Andrew's hand was cut to the bone. He and Robert were thrown into prison, where they lived on stale bread and water. When the boys came down with smallpox, their mother was allowed to take them from prison. Both Andrew's brother and mother died of the disease.

After the Revolution, Andrew drifted from relative to relative and attended several schools. Finally Jackson studied law and became a lawyer. He moved to what is now Tennessee and married a woman named Rachel Donelson Robards, whom he thought was divorced. Two years later the divorce was found to be unlawful, and Andrew remarried his wife.

When Tennessee became a state, Andrew became the first representative to Congress. When the War of 1812 broke out, Jackson began a military career that made him famous. His good cheer and willingness to share the hardships of his soldiers earned him the nickname Old Hickory. Other events in the war, such as his victory at the **Battle of New Orleans**, made him popular with many Americans.

Jackson's image as a rugged common man who loved horseracing and his plantation (called The Hermitage) helped make him a candidate for President. He ran unsuccessfully in 1824 but was elected in 1828. The campaign was a dirty one, and Jackson's marriage to Rachel when she had not really been divorced created a great scandal. Shortly afterward, Rachel died, and Andrew Jackson was sure that the scandal had killed her.

Andrew Jackson served as President for two terms and gave the office power it had not had since the days of Thomas Jefferson. He also made a number of changes in the way the nation's money was handled. On the darker side, he forced all the Indians living in the eastern part of the United States to move to reservations west of the Mississippi. A forceful, powerful, and popular man with many Americans, Andrew Jackson died at his Hermitage in 1845.

About Jackson County

Land and resources: Jackson County is made up of both level and very hilly land. There are many hardwood forests of oak and hickory. The county also has deposits of sand and gravel, clay, and shale. The Muscatatuck River and the East Fork of the White River make up the southern border of the county. The White also cuts through the county.

People and their work: Many farmers in the county raise livestock and poultry. Other people work in stores and offices. Many work in the county's factories, one of which processes spices and seasonings.

Facts to remember about Jackson County: The nation's first train robbery took place in Seymour in Jackson County in the fall of 1866. The Reno Gang, who lived in the county, stole $15,000. This probably gave other gangs, such as the famous James boys, the idea of robbing trains.

People probably chose to name their county after Andrew Jackson because of his leadership in the War of 1812. Many years later Jackson, known as Old Hickory, was elected President.

91

Jasper County

Named for: William Jasper
Date organized: 1838

William Jasper, a Revolutionary War hero, is believed to have been born in Georgetown, South Carolina. The Jasper family was split by the Revolutionary War. William's brother joined the British army, but William favored the Americans. When William and his friend, John Newton,* went to visit William's brother at the British camp where he was staying, they made a daring rescue of some American prisoners being held there. That exciting story is told on page 133.

In 1775 William joined the Continental army and became a sergeant. He was assigned to Fort Sullivan (now Fort Moultrie) in Charleston, South Carolina. In June of 1776 a British fleet opened fire on the fort, which was located on a small island. During the attack the flag was torn down. To those watching on shore, it looked as if the fort was lost to the British. But Jasper fixed the banner and raised it on a broken pole. Later he was rewarded for his bravery with a flag from the people of Charleston. Jasper pledged to defend it with his life.

William Jasper died before the Revolutionary War ended. He was killed October 9, 1779. Strangely enough, he was again

92

trying to raise the flag of a South Carolina infantry when he was shot.

*See Newton County.

About Jasper County

Land and resources: The land in Jasper County is level, with about 84 percent of it used for farming. There are some hardwood forests, which include oak and hickory trees. The county has deposits of peat, limestone, sand and gravel, as well as oil and gas. The Iroquois River flows through the county, and the Kankakee River forms the county's northern border.

People and their work: Farmers in Jasper County raise crops such as corn and soybeans. Other people work in stores, offices, and factories. About one third of Jasper's people work in other counties.

Facts to remember about Jasper County: Each fall thousands of sandhill cranes stop to rest in a wildlife area in the county. These large and beautiful birds are only some of the wildlife that live in this area.

Jay County

Named for: John Jay
Date organized: 1836

John Jay, the son of a wealthy merchant of Dutch background, was born on December 12, 1745, in New York. As a boy he had private teachers. Later he studied law at King's College, which is now Columbia University. Jay became a lawyer in 1768 and practiced in New York before he entered politics.

John Jay disagreed with many of the laws the British made for the colonists. Although he did not really want a revolution, he did support the American patriots. Because of his ability to speak for the American cause, Jay was sent to several countries to try to gain help for the American Revolution. Because of his travels, Jay did not get to sign the Declaration of Independence. However, the members of the Continental Congress chose him to be the president of this body in 1778.

John Jay was a believer in a strong central government. He was appointed by George Washington* to be the first **Chief Justice of the Supreme Court**. After holding that position for six years, he was elected governor of New York State. After two terms as governor, Jay retired. He died in 1829.

See Washington County.

94

About Jay County

Land and resources: Most of the land in Jay County is level. There are hardwood forests, which include oak, hickory, maple, beech, and birch. The county also has deposits of sand and gravel, oil and gas, as well as limestone. The Salamonie River flows through the northern half of the county.

People and their work: Over 80 percent of the county is made up of farmland, and farmers there raise oats and winter wheat along with other crops and livestock. Other people work in banks, stores, and in health service industries. Many go to work in the county's factories or go to jobs in other counties.

Facts to remember about Jay County: Natural gas was an important resource of the county in the late 1800s, and one of the county's cities, Dunkirk, was the "glass capital" of Indiana. Before the Civil War many slaves passed through the county in their journey on the **Underground Railroad.**

Jefferson County

Named for: Thomas Jefferson
Date organized: 1811

Thomas Jefferson, the third President of the United States, was born in Albemarle County, Virginia, on April 13, 1743. He attended school with his cousins at a schoolhouse on his father's plantation. In 1762 Thomas graduated from the College of William and Mary. Although he would have liked to become an architect or scientist, there was little demand for people of these skills in the Virginia colony. In 1767 he became a lawyer instead.

Thomas, tall with reddish hair, was popular with all who knew him. He was friendly and had a good sense of humor. He also had many talents. Socially he was a fine dancer, singer, and violinist. He used his knowledge of architecture and engineering to build his own home and plantation, Monticello.

Jefferson was interested in politics and served in the government of the Virginia colony. He believed that every man had a right to equal opportunity. He also believed that the thirteen colonies should rule themselves.

Jefferson joined a committee to plan a **document** that would give the colonies a government free of British rule. Because of his ability, Jefferson was chosen to do the actual writing. For eighteen days he worked on the document titled the Declaration of Independence. It was signed on July 4, 1776.

Jefferson served his state and country in many different positions. Among them was the governor of Virginia, Secretary of State under George Washington,* vice president under John Adams, and the third President of the United States.

After two terms as President, Jefferson retired to Monticello. There he enjoyed writing, farming, and inventing. Jefferson died on July 4th, exactly fifty years after the Declaration of Independence had been signed.

*See Washington County.

About Jefferson County

Land and resources: Hilly land makes up much of Jefferson County. A little more than half of the land is used for farming. Hardwood forests of oak, hickory, maple, beech, and birch are also common. The county has deposits of oil and gas, sand and gravel, limestone, and shale. The Ohio River forms the county's southern border. The Muscatatuck River cuts through its north-western section.

People and their work: Farmers in Jefferson County raise large crops of tobacco along with other crops such as corn, soybeans, and oats. Other people in the county are teachers and professional workers, such as lawyers. Some work in stores, factories, and tobacco warehouses.

<u>Facts to remember about Jefferson County:</u> Madison, Jefferson's county seat, was once the largest town in the state. Located on the banks of the Ohio River, it is also considered one of the most beautiful towns in the country and recalls the days when steamboats were a common sight on the river. Hanover College is located there.

This old photo shows steamboats being built at Madison. The invention of a practical steamboat by Robert Fulton in 1807 made travel possible both up and down the Ohio and Mississippi Rivers. The boats helped moved pioneers west, took farmers' crops to market, and delivered the products of industry far and wide.

Jennings County

Named for: Jonathan Jennings
Date organized: 1817

Jonathon Jennings, the first governor of Indiana, was born in New Jersey in 1784. His family soon moved to western Pennsylvania, where he spent most of his childhood. As a young man, he studied law in Jeffersonville, Indiana. In 1807 Jonathon set up his law practice in Vincennes. He later moved to Clark County.

Jennings was always interested in politics, and quickly became a popular candidate among the settlers. It was not unusual for him to work in the fields with the men during a campaign. He often took part in community activities, such as **log rolling**.

Jennings opposed slavery in the Indiana Territory. This position helped him win a race for territorial delegate to Congress and hold this office for three terms. He was also active in working to achieve statehood for Indiana.

In 1816 at the age of 32, Jennings was elected to be Indiana's first governor. He was also chosen to serve a second term but resigned so that he could run for representative to Congress. He was elected and served in that office until 1831.

Jennings' health began to fail in the 1830s. He received an appointment from President Jackson to make treaties with the

Indians, but that job did not last long. Jennings died at his home near Charleston, Indiana, on July 26, 1834.

About Jennings County

Land and resources: Low rolling hills cover much of Jennings County, and a little over half of it is used for farming. There are hardwood forests of oak, hickory, maple, beech, and birch. The county also has deposits of dolomite, limestone, gas, and shale oil. Sand Creek flows through the northwestern part of the county, while the Muscatatuck River forms part of the county's southern border.

People and their work: Farmers in the county produce poultry and eggs and grow corn. Other people in the county work in restaurants, banks, and stores. Some workers have jobs in factories, while others go to nearby counties to work.

Facts to remember about Jennings County: By 1860 two important roads and two important railroads crossed the county. This made Vernon, the county seat, an important transportation stop.

Johnson County

Named for: John Johnson
Date organized: 1822

John Johnson, a judge who served on the Indiana Supreme Court, was born in Kentucky. By the time he was a young man, he had settled in Vincennes, Indiana, where he practiced law. In 1805 he became involved in politics and served as a member of the Territorial Legislature. Johnson believed in slavery and thought slaves should be allowed in the Indiana Territory.

Part of Johnson's public work included being on a board that helped establish Vincennes University. Four others among these board members, John Gibson, Henry Vanderburgh, Benjamin Parke, and Francis Vigo, all had counties named for them. Johnson also had an important part in revising the laws of the territory.

Johnson's term in the Territorial House of Representatives ended in 1809. He was defeated by a man who opposed slavery. In 1816 Johnson was appointed as a judge in the Indiana Supreme Court. He served only a few months, however, before dying at his home in Knox County.

About Johnson County

Land and resources: Johnson County has level land except in the southwestern part, where there are hills. Over 85 percent of the land is used for farming, but there are also hardwood forests of oak, beech, maple, and some ash. The county also has deposits of limestone, dolomite, and shale. The White River and the Big Blue River run through corners of the county.

People and their work: Farmers in the county raise livestock and grow crops such as corn and soybeans. Other people work in stores, hospitals, and homes that take care of the elderly or disabled. Some work in factories that make such products as automobile parts. Many go to Indianapolis to work.

Facts to remember about Johnson County: The county has a huge, modern horse park, where all types of horse races and shows are held. Johnson County was home for two Indiana governors, Roger Branigan and Paul V. McNutt.

Hoosiers are proud of their many famous authors. James Whitcomb Riley (above) grew up in Hancock County and wrote poems about Hoosier life. Gene Stratton Porter (lower left) lived in Noble County, and Booth Tarkington (lower right) lived in Marion County.

The photo above shows the Central Indiana Canal in Marion County. The photo below shows a steamboat docked near a covered bridge on the National Road in Indianapolis.

Knox County

Named for: Henry Knox
Date organized: 1790

Henry Knox, the nation's first secretary of war, was born in Boston, Massachusetts, on July 25, 1750. At the age of nine, Henry quit school to work for a company that bound and sold books. Henry's large size and his willingness to start an argument won him a place as ringleader of Boston's "South End Gang." Each year his gang had a fight with the "North End Gang."

Henry educated himself by reading books that belonged to his boss. He was especially interested in military skills. By the time he was twenty, he opened his own bookstore.

Henry's knowledge of military skills was put to use during the Revolutionary War. Although his wife's parents wanted him to join the British army, Henry refused and joined the American colonists. During the war he fought in several famous battles. He also built forts. At one time he drew up and carried out a plan to move heavy guns and cannons that the Americans had captured from the British. Using sleds he and his men moved the valuable weapons from Fort Ticonderoga in what is now northern New York State to Boston, a 300-mile trip.

Henry's skills and knowledge won him the position of major general and chief of *artillery* in the Continental Army. At the end of the Revolutionary War, he became commander of the Continental Army. Later he was appointed secretary of war, in charge of both the army and the navy.

About Knox County

Land and resources: Knox County has both level land and low, rolling hills. There are hardwood forests of oak and hickory as well as a number of mineral deposits. These include oil and gas, sand and gravel, and coal. The Wabash River makes up the county's western border, while the White River forms its southern border and the West Fork of the White River its eastern border.

People and their work: Over 85 percent of the county is made up of farms, and farmers raise winter wheat, corn, soybeans, and hay. They are also famous for their peach and apple orchards. Many other people in the county are lawyers and teachers, while still others work in health businesses, stores, and factories.

Facts to remember about Knox County: The county seat, Vincennes, is the oldest town in Indiana and was built by French soldiers, traders, and settlers. Fort Sackville, which was located here, was the site of the famous American victory of George Rogers Clark over the British in the Revolutionary War. The city is also the site of an ancient Indian mound, which probably was built about 300 B.C. In more recent times, Vincennes was the birthplace of the famous comic Red Skelton.

Kosciusko County

Named for: Thaddeus Kosciuszko
Date organized: 1836

Born in Polish Lithuania in 1736, Thaddeus Kosciuszko studied in military schools in Poland and France. He was then urged by Benjamin Franklin to join the colonial forces in America. Thaddeus first served as an aide to General George Washington.* The American soldiers did not trust their foreign leader at first, but after a defeat by the British they began to listen to his advice. As time went by, Thaddeus became popular with them.

Kosciuszko's true talent lay in designing and building forts. He built several forts that were so strong the British could not take them. The Polish leader also fought many battles and helped the Americans gain independence from the British.

Kosciuszko was never paid for his services to America. Instead the American government invited him to become a citizen and offered him land and a pension. But Kosciuszko returned to his homeland with dreams of freeing it from Russian power and becoming the "George Washington" of Poland.

Poland was soon defeated. Kosciuszko was wounded and put into a Russian prison. Later he was freed and offered a post in the Russian army. He was also offered his old sword. He turned down both offers, stating, "I no longer need a sword, since I have no longer a country to defend." He died in Switzerland in 1817.

Indiana's people were so impressed by this Polish leader they named a county after him. The county seat was also named Warsaw, after the capital of Kosciuszko's native country.

See Washington County.

About Kosciusko County

Land and resources: Low hills cover the southern part of Kosciusko County, but level land makes up the largest section of the county. There are hardwood forests, which include oak, hickory, maple, birch, and beech trees. The county also has deposits of sand and gravel, marl, peat, and shale. The Tippecanoe River begins in the county. The many lakes in the area make it popular for recreation. One of them, Lake Wawasee, is the largest natural lake in Indiana.

People and their work: One of the county's farms is the world's largest producer of ducks. Other farmers in the county raise livestock, poultry, and hogs. They also grow crops such as corn, oats, hay, and soybeans. A large number of people work in the county's factories, which produce such items as hospital supplies and movie screens.

Facts to remember about Kosciusko County: Winona Lake in the central part of the county was a center for schools, camps, and cultural activities and was known as the **Chautauqua** of the Midwest. The famous preacher Billy Sunday had a home there.

LaGrange County

Named for: LaGrange-Bleneau
Date organized: 1832

LaGrange-Bleneau was the country home of Lafayette* and is located near the city of Paris, France. Grange is a French word which means "barn," but LaGrange-Bleneau was a splendid farm and castle. Its 800 acres were divided into gardens, vineyards, and woods. The three-story castle was made of dark stone and surrounded by a deep **moat**.

The castle once belonged to Lafayette's wife, Adrienne Francoise de Noailles. Her family was a very important one in France. The couple was married when she was only fourteen.

LaGrange was a busy, active place. All of Lafayette's grown children lived there with their families, and most of his grandchildren were born there. Because of Lafayette's ties with America, his American friends often visited the castle, which came to be known as the meeting place of the "Democracy of Two Worlds."

Lafayette's wife died at LaGrange in 1807, and Lafayette spent his remaining years there tending his crops and sheep. The castle still remains today, and Lafayette's 3,000-volume library is still in place.

*See Fayette County.

About LaGrange County

<u>Land and resources:</u> Most of the county has level land with a few low hills in the southern section. There are hardwood forests made up of oak, hickory, elm, ash, and cottonwood. The county also has deposits of sand and gravel, marl, peat, and shale. The Pigeon River runs through the northeast corner of the county, while the Little Elkhart River runs through the southwest corner.

<u>People and their work:</u> Farmers in the county raise livestock, producing large amounts of milk. They also grow oats and hay. Other people work in the county's factories, in offices, and in auto repair businesses.

<u>Facts to remember about LaGrange County:</u> Many Amish live in the county, running restaurants and giving tours of their farms and way of life. Thousands of visitors come to the auctions and flea markets in Shipshewana in the northern part of the county. Cattle and hogs are bought and sold as well as many unusual items such as wagon parts, old toys, and dishes.

Lake County

Named for: Lake Michigan
Date organized: 1836

Lake Michigan, whose tip forms the northwestern boundary of Indiana, is the only one of the Great Lakes to touch the state. It is also the only one of the Great Lakes lying totally within the borders of the United States. This makes it the largest body of fresh water in the nation. Its shoreline is 1,660 miles long. Only 45 of those miles lie in Indiana.

Lake Michigan was formed by **glaciers** about twenty thousand years ago during the great Ice Age. The glaciers moved slowly, gouging out huge holes in the earth's surface. When the climate grew warmer, the glaciers began to melt. The melting water ran across the land, making rivers and filling up the holes with water, forming lakes.

Lake Michigan is linked with the Atlantic Ocean by the St. Lawrence Seaway. Oceangoing ships can reach Lake Michigan by traveling up the St. Lawrence River, with its many canals and locks, and then passing through lakes Ontario, Erie, St. Clair, and Huron. The Straits of Mackinac connect Lake Huron with Lake Michigan. Rivers from Lake Michigan gradually make their way to the Mississippi River and into the Gulf of Mexico. One of the largest rivers that flows into Lake Michigan is the St. Joseph* River, which has its beginnings in Indiana.

111

The area around Lake Michigan has important ports, large industries, and recreation areas. Sportfishing is popular in the lake. The number of boats on the lake continues to grow each year. It is important that Indiana and the other states that surround Lake Michigan protect it from **pollution** so that its waters can be used and enjoyed for many years to come.

*See St. Joseph County.

About Lake County

Land and resources: Most of Lake County has level land, but unlike many Indiana counties, less than half of it is used for farming. There are some hardwood forests of oak and hickory. The county also has deposits of sand and gravel, peat, clay, lime, and shale. The Kankakee River forms the county's southern border, while the Little Calumet lies in the northwest section.
People and their work: Farmers in the county grow corn, soybeans, and vegetables. Other people in the county have jobs in the professions such as law and teaching. Still others work in stores and factories. Lake County's factories produce steel, hospital supplies, printing supplies, and other items. It is also the home of one of the largest oil refineries in the world.
Facts to remember about Lake County: Except for Marion County, Lake County has more people than any other Indiana county. The county is known for its large industrial cities and as the birthplace of Michael Jackson.

LaPorte County

Named for: The area's prairie
Date organized: 1832

When white explorers and traders first came to the Indiana region, they found thick forests. In what is now the northwestern part of the state, however, there were prairie openings. The French named one of these prairies *la porte*, meaning "door." At last they had found a passageway in a wilderness of giant forests!

The Door, or LaPorte, prairie was a small but welcome section of grassland surrounded by walls of forest. The prairie led west and allowed explorers a natural passage through fifteen miles of northern Indiana toward the prairies of Illinois and on to the Mississippi River.

In 1834 a journalist named Charles Fenno Hoffman rode on horseback to the forest opening. "It formed a door," he wrote, "opening upon an arm of the Grand Prairie which runs through the states of Indiana and Illinois and extends afterward, if I mistake not, to the base of the Rockys." There were other prairies in the area. Among them were Rolling Domain, Stillwell, and Hog.

About LaPorte County

<u>Land and resources:</u> Most of LaPorte County has level land except for some low hills in the northern sections. About 70 percent of the land is used for farming, and there are some hardwood forests of oak and hickory. The county also has deposits of sand and gravel, oil and gas, peat, and marl. The Kankakee River runs through the county.

<u>People and their work:</u> Farmers in the county raise dairy cattle and grow corn and other crops such as soybeans, oats, and winter wheat. Other people work in schools and colleges or are doctors and lawyers. A large number of people work in the county's factories, which produce cardboard boxes, rubber products, large electric fans, plastic containers, and other items.

<u>Facts to remember about LaPorte County:</u> Recreation is popular, with part of the county lying in the sand dune area of the Lake Michigan shore. There are also several small lakes where people can enjoy fishing and boating.

Lawrence County

Named for: James Lawrence
Date organized: 1818

James Lawrence, a naval hero, was born in Burlington, New Jersey, on October 1, 1781. The son of a lawyer, James joined the Navy before he was seventeen years old. Lawrence served on the schooner *Enterprise* and spent five years fighting pirates on the Barbary Coast. Because Lawrence was brave, Stephen Decatur* selected him to serve as his first lieutenant.

During the War of 1812, Lawrence commanded a warship called the *Hornet.* He captured an important British ship and was promoted to captain on a larger ship, the *Chesapeake.* The *Chesapeake* was ordered to attack British ships going to Canada. Before reaching Canada, however, the *Chesapeake* attacked a British ship trying to block Boston Harbor.

During the attack Lawrence was badly wounded. As he lay dying, he gave these instructions: "Tell the men to fire faster and not to give up the ship; fight her till she sinks." But the *Chesapeake* was too badly damaged and was forced to surrender. Lawrence's words lived on, however. Ever since, "Don't give up the ship" has been a famous slogan for sailors.

*See Decatur County.

About Lawrence County

<u>Land and resources:</u> Much of Lawrence County is made up of hilly land with forests of oak and hickory. The county has deposits of limestone, oil and gas, sandstone, clay, and shale. The East Fork of the White River winds through the county. Bluespring Caverns are also located in the county, with twenty miles of caves and fifteen miles of underground streams.

<u>People and their work:</u> Farmers in the county raise cattle and grow hay and apples. Other people work in offices, stores, and factories. Some work in the county's limestone quarries.

<u>Facts to remember about Lawrence County:</u> Limestone from Lawrence County has been used to build some of the nation's famous buildings, such as the Empire State Building in New York City. The county was also the boyhood home of one of the nation's first astronauts, Virgil (Gus) Grissom.

Madison County

Named for: James Madison
Date organized: 1823

James Madison, the fourth President of the United States, was born March 16, 1751, at Port Conway, Virginia. The oldest of ten children, James received a fine education. He attended the College of New Jersey (now Princeton University), where he was popular with the other students. Greatly interested in government, he helped form a club, the American Whig Society, whose members discussed political issues.

After leaving college, James became involved in politics, and helped his young and struggling country in many ways. In 1779 he was elected to the Continental Congress. He believed that the colonists should govern themselves and helped write the Constitution. Madison later became known as the Father of the Constitution.

Madison married Dolley Payne Todd, a widow known for her charm. When James was made Secretary of State under Thomas Jefferson,* Dolley acted as the hostess for the capital since both Jefferson's wife and the wife of Vice President Aaron Burr were dead. When Madison was elected President after Jefferson, Dolley became the true first lady. During the second term of Madison's office, the War of 1812 was being waged.

The British captured Washington, D.C., and burned it. Dolley saved some important papers and also a portrait of George Washington.**

By the end of Madison's second term, the United States was at peace and there was a great westward expansion. James Madison left office a very popular man. He went home to Virginia and helped Jefferson found the University of Virginia. He died on June 28, 1836, at the age of 85.

*See Jefferson County.
**See Washington County.

About Madison County

Land and resources: Madison County is made up largely of level land. Over three fourths of it is used for farming. There are hardwood forests of maple, beech, and birch. The county also has deposits of oil and gas, peat, dolomite, and limestone. The White River flows through the county.

People and their work: Farmers in the county raise large crops of soybeans and tomatoes. A large number of people work in stores and factories. The county's factories make such products as automobile parts, glass, cabinets, and cardboard boxes.

Facts to remember about Madison County: Several burial mounds of early Indian civilizations can be found near Anderson, the county seat. Later the area was the home of a Delaware Indian village. The city was named for a Delaware chief, Kikthawenund, also known as Captain Anderson. In the late 1800s, large amounts of natural gas were taken from wells near Anderson, and it was known as the Queen of the Gas Belt.

Marion County

Named for: Francis Marion
Date organized: 1822

Born in Winyah, South Carolina, in 1732, Francis Marion, an army hero, was the youngest of five boys. As a child he was small and sickly. His mother made him rest and take bitter medicines when he wanted to be playing war games and taking part in corn cob fights with his brothers. Little by little he began to be strong.

Swamplands were Francis's favorite places. He became skillful at hunting alligators and snakes. By the time he was ten, Francis could paddle and pole a boat into the swamp and fire his father's musket.

As a young man, Francis joined the South Carolina state militia and fought in battles against the Cherokee Indians. When there were no battles to be fought, he was a planter on land near the Santee River in South Carolina.

Marion was a lieutenant colonel in the South Carolina militia when the Revolutionary War began. He organized soldiers and taught them to fight like Indians. Two of his men were William Jasper* and John Newton.** The men soon became skillful at quick raids against the British. He and his men would appear from nowhere, attack, and then disappear into the swamps. His style of fighting earned him the nickname Swampfox. His small band of men wore a white feather in their caps.

After the Revolutionary War Francis Marion worked as a planter. He also served several terms in the South Carolina senate and helped write the state constitution. He died in 1795.

*See Jasper County.
**See Newton County.

About Marion County

Land and resources: Most of Marion County is made up of level land. There are some forests of oak, hickory, maple, birch, and beech. The county also has deposits of sand and gravel, oil and gas, limestone, shale, and clay. The West Fork of the White River flows through the county.

People and their work: Only about one fourth of the land is used for farming, and farmers grow crops such as vegetables and nursery products such as shrubs and plants. Most of the people work in offices, stores, museums, and in state government jobs. Some people work in plants that process meat and in factories that make drugs, paper, furniture, television sets, and records.

Facts to remember about Marion County: The county is the home of Indianapolis, Indiana's largest city and state capital. The city is famous for the Indy 500, an automobile race held here each year. The city is also the home of outstanding museums, including the Indianapolis Children's Museum, the largest of its kind in the world.

Marshall County

Named for: John Marshall
Date organized: 1836

John Marshall, Chief Justice of the United States for thirty-four years, was born September 24, 1755, in Germantown, Pennsylvania. The oldest of fifteen children, John was educated by private tutors. His father directed John's reading and purchased a set of law books which John began to study.

When John was eighteen his education was interrupted by the American Revolution. He served as an officer and took part in many major battles. In 1780 he resigned from the army and became a lawyer. He began his practice in Richmond, Virginia, and became one of the state's leading lawyers.

John Marshall began his political career by serving as a state lawmaker in Virginia. In 1799 he was elected to represent Virginia in the House of Representatives. He then served as Secretary of State under President John Adams. He became Chief Justice of the United States Supreme Court in 1801 and held the office until he died in 1835. He served in that job longer than any other person and helped give the Supreme Court the power it has today.

Marshall died from injuries he received in a stagecoach accident. The nation mourned his death and the Liberty Bell in

Philadelphia was rung at his funeral. It was then that the famous bell cracked.

About Marshall County

Land and resources: Marshall County has mostly level land with a few areas of low, rolling hills. About 80 percent of the land is used for farming, and there are hardwood forests of oak and hickory. The county also has deposits of sand and gravel, oil and gas, peat, and marl. The Tippecanoe River runs through the county's southeastern corner.

People and their work: Farmers in the county raise many dairy cattle and grow hay, corn, and other crops. Other people in the county are teachers or work in stores and factories.

Facts to remember about Marshall County: Near Plymouth, the county seat, was a Potawatomi village headed by a chief named Menominee. When Menominee refused to turn his village over to whites, Indiana Governor David Wallace sent General John Tipton with soldiers to drive out the Potawatomi. Menominee and his people were forced to go to a reservation in Kansas, and many of them died on the long, hard journey. Today a monument honors Menominee where his village once stood.

Martin County

Named for: Uncertain
Date organized: 1820

There is no certainty about the person for whom Martin County was named. Several people may have had this honor. One source names Major Martin of Newport, Kentucky. Other sources list Major Thomas Martin or John P. Martin. Perhaps the real answer lies buried with the people who named the county.

Unless two men of importance in the region were named John P. Martin, the last is an unlikely guess. A Kentucky county was named for this man in 1870. But this John P. Martin would have been only a child in 1820.

There were two Thomas Martins who may have been the "correct" Martin. The first, Thomas Martin of Newport, Kentucky, was a major in the Continental army during the American Revolution. He died in 1818, two years before this Indiana county was named.

The second Thomas Martin was Thomas E. Martin. He was born about 1775 and was living within the county's borders when it was formed. According to an 1820 census, this Martin owned land in Columbia Township and lived there with his wife and family. He served as one of the first road bosses and was in charge of caring for the road from Hindostan to French Lick.

(Hindostan was a town that was abandoned in the late 1820s because its citizens died of a strange disease.)

Whoever the real Martin was, early county residents must have thought him to be a person who helped the growth of his region or nation.

About Martin County

Land and resources: Martin is a hilly county with many forests and mineral resources. The hardwood forests are made up largely of oak and hickory, with some maple, beech, and ash. The county has deposits of oil and gas, sand and gravel, coal, **gypsum**, sandstone, and clay. The East Fork of the White River flows through the county, and there are at least ten caves located in the area. The county also has one of the state's large lakes, Lake Greenwood.

People and their work: Most of the county's people work in stores, restaurants, gas stations, factories, and mines. There are fewer farmers here than in most parts of Indiana, but they raise hogs and cattle and grow corn and hay.

Facts to remember about Martin County: The county is a place of beautiful forests, waterfalls, streams, and **bluffs**. It has both state and national forest areas for people to enjoy. A legend says that Indians hid silver in one of the county's caves.

Miami County

Named for: Miami Indians
Date organized: 1834

Miami County is located in the heart of what was once a great Miami empire. The Miami Indians, a gentle farming people, had villages in the region that is now Indiana, western Ohio, southern Michigan, and eastern Illinois. They raised corn, pumpkins, squash, beans, sunflowers, and other crops. They also ate fish and wild foods such as roots, nuts, and berries.

The Miami villages, like the villages of other Indian tribes, were gradually broken down and destroyed. There were wars with their enemies on the east, the Iroquois, and their enemies on the west, the **Sioux**. But most harmful was the arrival of people from Europe. Their diseases, such as smallpox and measles, killed thousands of Indian people. The alcohol that the whites traded to the Indians for furs and land helped destroy the Indian way of life.

One of the great Miami leaders was Little Turtle. Fighting with Ojibwa, Potawatomi, and his own warriors, Little Turtle won more battles against the whites than any other Indian leader. When the United States Government sent General Anthony Wayne* and larger armies to the Northwest Territory, Little Turtle realized his Indian forces would lose and urged them to make peace treaties. His warriors fought anyway and lost to Wayne.

In the years between 1795 and 1827 the Miami signed treaties that gave nearly all their land to the American settlers. Except for a few who remained on a small reservation in Wabash County, the Indians were sent to Kansas. The blizzards of winter and homesickness caused the deaths of nearly half of these people. Many tried to return to Indiana.

The Miami and other Indians were later pushed off their reservation land in Kansas. As white settlers moved further west, they decided they wanted that Indian land, too. The remaining Miami were sent to Oklahoma in 1867.

See Wayne County.

About Miami County

Land and resources: Miami County has both level land and some low, rolling hills. Over 80 percent of it is used for farming. The county has some oak and hickory forests. It also has deposits of oil and gas, sand and gravel, dolomite, and limestone. The Eel River and the Wabash River run through the county.

People and their work: Farmers in Miami County raise cattle and hogs and grow crops such as corn and hay. Other people in the county work in health service jobs, stores, and factories.

Facts to remember about Miami County: One of the nation's finest circuses, the Hagenbeck-Wallace Circus, began in Peru, the Miami County seat. It began in the late 1800s and still exists today. The county is also the home of the famous songwriter, Cole Porter.

Monroe County

Named for: James Monroe
Date organized: 1818

James Monroe, the fifth President of the United States, was born on April 28, 1758, in Westmoreland County, Virginia. The oldest of five children, James went to a private school. When he was sixteen years old he entered William and Mary College in Williamsburg. Before he had finished, the American Revolution began and James joined a Virginia regiment. Because he was an expert rifleman and horseman, he had become an officer of high rank by the end of the war.

After the Revolution, James studied law and held several different jobs in Virginia's state government. In 1803 President Thomas Jefferson* sent him to France. There Monroe was able to convince the French leader, Napoleon, to sell the great **Louisiana Territory** to the United States. Monroe considered that the greatest accomplishment of his career. Under President James Madison,** Monroe served as Secretary of State and then Secretary of War. In 1816 he was elected President.

Monroe was a popular President, and his two terms were known a time of peace and growth. Five new states entered the Union during that time. During his second term he issued the

127

Monroe Doctrine. This was a warning to European countries that they could no longer open new colonies on the American continents or send armies into American nations.

After two terms as President, Monroe retired. He died on July 4, 1831, in New York City. He was the third President to die on Independence Day.

See Jefferson County.
**See Madison County.*

About Monroe County

Land and resources: Monroe County is made up largely of rolling hills. There are some hardwood forests of oak and hickory. The county also has deposits of oil and gas, gypsum, and limestone. Monroe Lake covers a large section of the southeast corner of the county.

People and their work: A large number of people are teachers or have jobs with the county's schools or with Indiana University in Bloomington. There are also many people in professional jobs, such as doctors and lawyers. The county has much fewer farmers than most other counties in the state.

Facts to remember about Monroe County: The county's limestone quarries helped Bloomington and the surrounding area to grow. Today Indiana University, one of the nation's outstanding state universities, has about 33,000 students and has an important influence on life in Monroe County.

Montgomery County

Named for: Richard Montgomery
Date organized: 1823

Richard Montgomery, a leader in the Revolutionary War, was born near Dublin, Ireland, on December 2, 1738. He went to college and in 1756 entered the British army. After spending several years in the army, Montgomery decided to move to America. He bought a farm in Rhinebeck, New York, and married Janet Livingston.

Even though he had lived in Great Britain much of his life, Montgomery adopted the views of the colonists and agreed that they should free themselves from Britain. With his army experience, he quickly became a brigadier general in the colonial army. Replacing the sick General Schuyler, he captured the British fort at Montreal. Since it was difficult to get and keep soldiers in the colonial army, Montgomery often had to bribe them. He gave them his own goods to keep them in the fight. Some of these goods included "a watch, a great coat, a jacket, breeches, stockings, shoes, shirt, caps, mittens, socks, and money."

Montgomery lost his life in the Americans' struggle for freedom. He was killed in an attack on Quebec on December 31, 1775. He is buried at St. Paul's Church in New York City.

About Montgomery County

Land and resources: Low, rolling hills cover much of the county except in the north and in some eastern areas. There are some forests of oak and hickory. The county also has deposits of sand and gravel, clay, and shale. Sugar Creek, one of the most scenic streams in the state, runs through the county on its way to join the Wabash.

People and their work: About 80 percent of Montgomery's land is used for farming, and farmers raise hogs and grow corn and soybeans. Some of the county's people are teachers or work in offices. Others work in factories that produce such items as travel trailers, nails, and fences.

Facts to remember about Montgomery County: The county is often called the literary center of Indiana, since so many authors have lived and worked in Crawfordsville, the county seat. One of them was General Lew Wallace, a Civil War general, who wrote *Ben Hur*. Wabash College is also located in Crawfordsville. Montgomery County is known for its beautiful state parks.

Morgan County

Named for: Daniel Morgan
Date organized: 1822

Daniel Morgan was born in New Jersey in the winter of 1736. His mother died when he was a boy and Daniel worked with his father, running an iron furnace. At sixteen he left home to find a better life on the western frontier of Virginia. There he worked first as a **teamster** and then as a **wagon master.**

During the French and Indian War Morgan used his skill as a teamster for General Edward Braddock. He also organized his own group of riflemen from Virginia to fight the French and their Indian allies. In 1758 he was shot by an Indian and lost the teeth on the left side of his mouth.

Morgan married Abigail Baily and bought a farm the couple named Soldiers' Rest. But it was seldom a resting place for Morgan who organized another company of soldiers when the American Revolution began. In one battle he and his men joined other American soldiers in an attack against the British in Quebec. The Americans were defeated and forced to surrender. Morgan was so upset that he wept. He was also taken prisoner, but he was later released.

Morgan's leadership did not go unnoticed. He became a colonel and led five hundred sharpshooters known as Morgan's

Rangers. He was then promoted to brigadier general and commanded one thousand men. One of his victories, the Battle of Cowpens, was a turning point in the war. But Morgan was forced to retire from active duty because of his health.

After the Revolution, Morgan served in the United States Congress. He also had time to spend at Soldiers' Rest. By the time of his death in 1802, he owned thousands of acres of land.

About Morgan County

Land and resources: Morgan County has areas of both level and hilly land, with about half of it used for farming. There are forests of oak and hickory. The county also has deposits of sand and gravel, sandstone, clay, shale, and limestone. The West Fork of the White River crosses the county.

People and their work: A large number of the county's people go to Indianapolis in Marion County or Bloomington in Monroe County to work. Others work in stores, auto repair shops, and factories. The county's farmers raise hogs and grow such crops as corn and soybeans.

Facts to remember about Morgan County: A fishery in the county raises goldfish — perhaps more than any other hatchery in the world.

Newton County

Named for: John Newton
Date organized: 1835

The first name chosen for Newton County was Beaver County. However, a decision was made to name it instead in honor of John Newton. Newton, a hero in the Revolutionary War, was born in Charleston, South Carolina. All that is known of his life is closely connected to the life of his friend, William Jasper.*

John Newton and William Jasper went to visit Jasper's brother, a soldier stationed in a British army camp during the American Revolution. William Jasper did not feel the same loyalty toward the British as his brother. At the camp, William felt sorry for American prisoners who were chained and being taken to Georgia. The wife and baby of one of the prisoners was with the group. The woman's grief over the possibility that her husband would be killed moved William Jasper to action. He secretly convinced Newton that they must free the prisoners.

Newton and Jasper said goodbye to Jasper's brother and other British soldiers. Then they circled ahead to the next camping place and hid. When the soldiers arrived and put down their guns to rest, Newton and Jasper grabbed two muskets and began shooting. The guards who weren't killed or wounded surrendered. Newton and Jasper released the American prisoners and made prisoners of the British guards.

Later in the war John Newton was taken prisoner by the British. He died soon afterward of smallpox.

See Jasper County.

About Newton County

Land and resources: The county is made up of nearly all level land. There are hardwood forests of oak and hickory. The county also has deposits of limestone, sand and gravel, shale, peat, and oil. The Kankakee River forms the county's northern border, and the Iroquois River runs through the southern section of the county.

People and their work: Most of the county is used for farming, and farmers raise poultry and grow corn. Some also grow mint, which is made into an oil to flavor candy, gum, and teas. Many people work in banks and offices, while others work in the county's factories.

Facts to remember about Newton County: In 1679 the famous French explorer Robert, Sieur de La Salle probably went down the Kankakee to the Illinois River. George Ade, a famous humorist and playwright, lived on a farm near Brook in Newton County.

Noble County

Named for: James Noble
Date organized: 1836

It was long thought that Noble County was named for Noah Noble, who served as Indiana's governor from 1831 to 1837. History experts have changed their minds about this, however. It is now believed that the county was named for Noah's older brother, James. James Noble was born in Virginia in the 1780s. When he was young, his family moved to Newport, Kentucky.

As an adult, James Noble moved to Ohio. There he married a girl from Ireland named Mary Lindsey. Soon after his marriage James began to study law. He began his practice in Lawrenceburg, Ohio. He also operated a ferry across the Ohio River.

The Noble family, which eventually included six children, moved to Brookville, Indiana, in the southeastern part of the state. There James set up another law practice and in time became one of the best lawyers in the region. He was also a colonel in the Indiana militia.

When Indiana became a state in 1816, James Noble was elected to the United States Senate. An excellent speaker, Noble served as a Senator for fifteen years. He died in office in 1831.

135

His wife died in 1839, the same year that Noble County was organized.

About Noble County

<u>Land and resources:</u> The county has some level land and some low, rolling hills. About three fourths of the land is used for farming. There are hardwood forests of oak, hickory, maple, beech, and birch. There are also deposits of sand and gravel, oil and gas, marl, shale, and peat. The Elkhart River flows through the county. There are also nine lakes that naturally connect with each other along with two others in same area. They are part of a park called Chain O'Lakes State Park.

<u>People and their work:</u> Farmers in Noble County raise dairy cattle and grow crops such as oats, corn, and soybeans. Other people work in health service jobs or in factories. Some go to other counties to work.

<u>Facts to remember about Noble County:</u> Wildflower Woods along Sylvan Lake in the county is a state memorial to Indiana writer Gene Stratton Porter. She and her husband owned land along the lake, where she photographed, painted, and wrote about nature.

Ohio County

Named for: the Ohio River
Date organized: 1844

According to the records of an early missionary, the Ohio River received its name from a Miami* Indian word. The Miami called it the *Oyo*, or *Ohi*, or perhaps *Ohiopeekhanne*. The early French explorers called the Ohio River *La Belle Riviere*, or "beautiful river." The Indian name, too, probably meant "beautiful river."

The Ohio River begins where the Allegheny River meets the Monongahela River at the city of Pittsburgh, Pennsylvania. It flows northwest in Pennsylvania for about twenty miles and then swings southwest until it reaches the Mississippi River at Cairo, Illinois. It forms the southern boundary of both Ohio and Indiana. Including the length of the Allegheny River, the Ohio is 1,306 miles long. Other large rivers, such as the Wabash River in Indiana, flow into the Ohio.

Perhaps the first European to see the Ohio River was Robert, Sieur de La Salle, the French explorer. About 1669 La Salle explored areas of what is now Indiana. His writings describe a great river that surely was the Ohio. He traveled along the river for some distance. Because of his explorations, the king of France claimed all the Ohio Valley for France. During the French and Indian War, this area was captured and claimed by the English.

137

The river has played an important part in the development of the Midwest. The Indians used it as a highway, as did the settlers who were led into the Ohio Valley by Daniel Boone.** For some time in the 1800s it was a dividing line between slavery and freedom for black people.

Today the river has changed. Once its banks were lined with farms, and river barges carried farm produce as far south as New Orleans. Today there are many steel mills, chemical plants, oil refineries, and electric power plants along the river banks. And modern river barges carry steel, oil, coal, chemicals, and other items for industry.

*See Miami County.
**See Boone County.

About Ohio County

Land and resources: Most of the land in Ohio County is hilly. There are hardwood forests of oak, hickory, maple, birch, and beech. The county also has deposits of sand and gravel. The Ohio River forms the county's eastern boundary, and Laughtery Creek forms the northern boundary.

People and their work: Farmers in the county raise livestock and tobacco. A large number of the county's people go to neighboring counties to work. Others work in stores, health service businesses, and factories.

Facts to remember about Ohio County: Ohio County is the smallest county in Indiana.

Orange County

Named for: Orange County, North
Carolina
Date organized: 1816

The people who settled in this part of Indiana wanted to remember the place from which many of them came. That was Orange County, North Carolina. It had been named for William of Orange, King of England, who was born in Holland in 1650. His father died just before William was born, and his mother died when he was ten. He was raised by his grandmother and uncle.

The House of Orange was popular with the people in Holland. But other provinces ruled by them were jealous. Young Prince William learned early that he had enemies, and he learned to hide his thoughts and feelings.

When William became ruler of Holland he lost many battles to the French. But the military skills he lacked he made up for in marriage. He married Mary, who was next in line to become Queen of England. The royal couple was urged by many English citizens to overthrow the king still in power, King James. William agreed, and he and his army marched into London. They were joined by **rebels** of King James's army. James fled to France, leaving William and Mary as rulers.

139

William and Mary improved life for the English people. They gave citizens more rights, such as freedom of the press and freedom to choose their own religion. William died in 1702 at the age of 51.

About Orange County

Land and resources: Orange County is made up of hilly land and many forests of oak and hickory. Its also has deposits of oil and gas, limestone, and gypsum. The Patoka River winds through much of the southern part of the county. There are fifty-seven known caves in the county.

People and their work: Less than half of the county's land is in farms, but the farmers who are there raise corn and livestock. Other people have jobs in hotels, recreation areas, stores, and factories. One of the factories makes the famous Kimball pianos.

Facts to remember about Orange County: The county is known for its beauty and its resort city of French Lick, which began as a French fur trading post. People later came here to bathe in the waters of the mineral springs, which they thought would improve their health. Today there are many other attractions, including skiing in the winter. Basketball star Larry Bird is from Orange County.

Owen County

Named for: Abraham Owen
Date organized: 1819

Not much is known about the early life of Abraham Owen except that he was born in Prince Edward County in Virginia. At the age of sixteen he moved with his family to Kentucky. As settlers moved into the Northwest Territory, Owen took part in battles against the Indians. He also became a surveyor. Later he was elected to serve in the state government of Kentucky.

It was Owen's death that probably caused the people of Owen County to choose his name for their county. When Owen heard that William Henry Harrison* was raising an army to fight Indians, he went to Vincennes, Indiana, to join the fight. He served as Harrison's aide and rode north with him to Tippecanoe.** He died in the battle with the Indians there.

There are several stories about Owen's death. One says that he was riding Harrison's white horse and was quickly attacked by the Indians, who thought they were killing the leader. Another account says Owen brought his own white horse from Kentucky and was simply killed as he rode into battle. He died on November 7, 1811.

141

The people of Owen County also chose to honor another soldier in the Battle of Tippecanoe. They named the county seat after Captain Spier Spencer,*** who was also killed in that conflict.

*See Harrison County.
**See Tippecanoe County.
***See Spencer County.

About Owen County

Land and resources: The county is made up of both level and hilly land, with less than half of it used for farming. There are forests of oak and hickory, and the White River winds its way across the county. The county has deposits of oil and gas, coal, sand and gravel, limestone, and gypsum. There are about ten caves in the county.

People and their work: Farmers in Owen County raise largely corn and soybeans. Over half of the county's workers go to neighboring counties to work. Others have jobs in factories and stores.

Facts to remember about Owen County: The Lafayette and Jeffersonville Turnpike, a major Indiana road, crossed the county in the early 1800s. Still, not many people settled in the area, and today Owen has a small population. In the northern part of the county Indiana's largest waterfall, Cataract Falls, tumbles into Cataract Lake.

Parke County

Named for: Benjamin Parke
Date organized: 1821

Benjamin Parke was born on September 2, 1777, in New Jersey and grew up on a farm there. When he was about twenty years old, he traveled west to Lexington, Kentucky. There he studied law and became a lawyer. In 1801 Parke moved into the Indiana Territory, living first at Vincennes in what is now Knox County and then at Salem in the present Washington County.

Benjamin Parke served in many jobs as Indiana moved toward statehood. In 1805 he was sent to the United States Congress as a **delegate**. President Thomas Jefferson* appointed him to be a judge in the territory. Parke also worked on forming the state's constitution and helped make a good educational system for the new state. He also served as an Indian agent and helped write several land treaties with the Indians.

When Indiana became a state, Parke served as a district judge. He had to ride long distances on horseback to settle cases. Once he rode completely across the state to try a man for stealing a 25-cent pocketknife.

Parke was very interested in education and had one of the largest private libraries in Indiana. He helped Vincennes

Library and Vincennes University grow and become successful institutions. He founded the state law library, now called the Library of the Supreme Court. He also organized the Indiana Historical Society and was its first president.

See Jefferson County.

About Parke County

Land and resources: Parke County has level land, some low, rolling hills, and a few areas of steep hills. Some of the land is covered with hardwood forests of oak and hickory. About two thirds of it is used for farming. The county also has deposits of sand and gravel, coal, clay, and shale. The Wabash River forms the county's western boundary, while Sugar Creek cuts across the northern part of the county.

People and their work: Farmers in the county grow soybeans and corn and raise cattle. Many people work in restaurants, stores, banks, and factories. Some go to other counties to work.

Facts to remember about Parke County: There are about thirty - four covered bridges remaining in the county, more than in any other county in the nation. Many of them were built in the 1800s.

Perry County

Named for: Oliver Hazard Perry
Date organized: 1818

Oliver Hazard Perry, a Naval hero, was born on August 23, 1785, in South Kingston, Rhode Island. His family loved the sea. At one time there were seven of them attending the Naval Academy in Annapolis, Maryland. Oliver, too, attended the Naval Academy and at the age of fourteen joined the United States Navy.

In the Navy, Oliver served under his father, Christopher Raymond Perry. Oliver fought pirates on the Barbary Coast of North Africa. He also fought in the West Indies in what was called the War against Tripoli. By the time he was twenty-two, he had earned the rank of lieutenant.

During the War of 1812, Oliver was sent to the Great Lakes. There he oversaw the building of a fleet of ships. Using lumber from the forests along Lake Erie, he and his men built eight ships. By the fall of 1813 they were ready to meet the enemy.

Oliver Perry and his fleet met British ships near Put In Bay, off the shores of Ohio. The fighting was so fierce between the ships that 83 of the 101 men on Perry's ship were killed. Perry escaped over the side of his ship and rowed to another. The battle continued until the British surrendered, giving the United States control of Lake Erie. Perry sent his now-famous message to American troops on the Ohio shore: "We have met the enemy and they are ours."

Oliver Hazard Perry reached the rank of commodore and spent the years after the War of 1812 fighting pirates. In 1819 he became ill with yellow fever. He died in Trinidad in the West Indies at the age of thirty-four.

About Perry County

<u>Land and resources:</u> Most of Perry County has hilly land, much of it covered with forests of oak and hickory. The county has deposits of coal, oil and gas, sand and gravel, clay, sandstone, and limestone. The Ohio River forms the county's southern boundary. Part of the county's western boundary is formed by the Anderson River as it flows to the Ohio.

<u>People and their work:</u> Farmers in the county raise corn and cattle. Other people work in stores, banks, and factories, several of which make furniture. Some workers have jobs in the county's coal mines.

<u>Facts to remember about Perry County:</u> A large cotton mill in the county once employed about 400 workers and produced thread and cloth from raw cotton. During the Civil War, workers at the mill made Union Army uniforms. The county has national forest lands where people can backpack for several days along miles of marked trails.

Pike County

Named for: Zebulon Pike
Date organized: 1817

Zebulon Montgomery Pike, an army officer and explorer, was born in Lamberton, New Jersey, on January 5, 1779. His father was a captain in George Washington's army. By the time he was fifteen, Zeb had joined the army and become part of his father's regiment. Five years later, he became an officer.

After the United States bought the Louisiana Territory from France, Pike was sent up the Mississippi River on several trips. He was to explore the river and purchase land from the Indians for future forts. He was also to be sure that Canadian traders understood that the land now belonged to the United States.

Pike's second trip was to explore the Arkansas and Red rivers and make a map of the southern border of the Louisiana Territory. Pike started his trip in July and did not reach Colorado until late fall. He and his men had only light clothing and were not prepared for the cold weather in the Rocky Mountains. Pike was especially impressed with a great blue peak rising above the other mountains. The peak was named Pike's Peak in honor of the man who found it.

While exploring the Red River, Pike accidentally wandered into Spanish territory. He was arrested and taken to Mexico. He was released the following summer.

Pike served during the War of 1812 and was a brigadier general. While he was leading an attack against the British at York, Canada, some ammunition exploded and Pike was killed. He was only thirty-four years old.

About Pike County

Land and resources: The land in Pike County is made up largely of low hills. Unlike many Indiana counties, less than half of the land is used for farming. There are many hardwood forests of oak, hickory, elm, ash, and cottonwood trees. The county also has deposits of oil and gas, coal, limestone, shale, and clay. The East Fork of the White River forms the county's northern boundary. The Patoka River also flows through the county.

People and their work: Farmers in the county raise cattle and grow corn and soybeans. A large number of workers go to jobs in other counties. Others work in Pike's restaurants, banks, and factories.

Facts to remember about Pike County: Petersburg, the county seat, was an important stop on an early road known as the Vincennes Trace and also on the Wabash and Erie Canal. A coal mine near Petersburg in Pike County was an important "station" for the Underground Railroad. This secret chain of hiding places was for slaves escaping north to freedom before the Civil War. Many of Indiana's people helped the slaves and kept them in stations, or hiding places, during daylight hours.

Porter County

Named for: David Porter
Date organized: 1836

David Porter was born in Boston, Massachusetts, on February 1, 1780. His family loved the sea, and both his father and his uncle commanded ships during the American Revolution. By the time David was sixteen, he was traveling with his father. Twice he was forced onto British ships, but each time he managed to escape.

When he was eighteen, David was serving on ships without his father and building his naval career. He served in New Orleans and then in the War of 1812. He captured several British ships but was eventually overpowered by British ships and was forced to surrender.

After the War of 1812, Porter served on a board of naval commissioners. He was also sent to the West Indies to command ships there which were trying to overcome pirates. While he was in Puerto Rico one of his men was insulted by Spanish officials. Without authority from the United States Government, Porter demanded that the Spanish apologize. For this, Porter was ordered home and suspended from the Navy for six months.

Porter was angry and resigned from the United States Navy. He then joined the Mexican Navy and served as its commander in chief for three years. Later, President Andrew Jackson*

149

appointed him to several positions in the United States government. Porter died in 1843.

See Jackson County.

About Porter County

Land and resources: Most of Porter County is made up of level land with over half of it used for farming. There are hardwood forests of oak and hickory. The county also has deposits of sand and gravel, clay, shale, and peat. The Kankakee River forms the southern boundary of the county.

People and their work: Many of the farmers in the county raise crops such as soybeans, corn, and oats. They also raise vegetables, such as sweet corn and tomatoes, and nursery and greenhouse products. Some people work in stores and factories or are teachers. Many go to neighboring counties to work.

Facts to remember about Porter County: The county is the headquarters of the Indiana Dunes National Lakeshore. Here the federal government tries to protect miles of beautiful sand dunes along Lake Michigan. All around the park lie industrial areas with heavy air and water pollution.

Posey County

Named for: *Thomas Posey*
Date organized: 1814

Thomas Posey, a governor of the Indiana Territory for several years, was born on July 9,1750, in Fairfax County, Virginia. He was a neighbor and close friend of George Washington.* Later when a county was named in Posey's honor, the county seat was named Mt. Vernon. That name was chosen because of Posey's friendship with George Washington.

Posey was a soldier most of his early life. He was an officer in the American Revolution and fought in many important battles, two of them with General Anthony Wayne.** When the war was over, he helped Wayne fight Indians in the Northwest Territory.

Posey began a career in politics in the early 1800s. He served in the Kentucky senate and then became lieutenant governor of Kentucky from 1806 to 1809. He then moved to Louisiana and in 1812 was elected to the United States Senate, representing the newly-created state of Louisiana.

In 1813 Posey left the Senate to become governor of the Indiana Territory. Posey was not very popular because he wanted Indiana to be a slave state. When Indiana entered the Union as a free state Posey ran first for Congress and then for governor. Both times he was defeated by men who opposed slavery. Posey died in 1818 while serving as an Indian agent in Illinois.

See Washington County.
**See Wayne County.*

About Posey County

Land and resources: Located in the southwestern corner of the state, Posey County is made up mostly of rolling hills with over 80 percent of it used for farming. The county has forests of oak and hickory and deposits of oil and gas, sand and gravel, and coal. The Ohio River forms the southern boundary of the county, while the eastern boundary of the county is formed by the Wabash River.

People and their work: Farmers in the county raise winter wheat, corn, and soybeans. Other people work as doctors or teachers or have jobs in stores and factories. Still others have jobs in neighboring counties.

Facts to remember about Posey County: The county is the home of New Harmony, a settlement begun in the early 1800s. It was made up of artists, writers, and social reformers who wished to build an ideal community. Their experiment failed, but New Harmony still remains famous for the efforts made there.

Pulaski County

Named for: Casimir Pulaski
Date organized: 1839

Casimir Pulaski was born in Podolia, Poland, on March 4, 1748. While still a young man he took part in an attempt to overthrow the Polish king. He was forced from his country and went to Paris, France. There he met Benjamin Franklin,* who was trying to persuade the French to help the Americans in their War of Independence. Pulaski became interested in the American cause and came to America to become a soldier.

From the beginning, Pulaski had no difficulty proving that he was a fine soldier. He was made a brigadier general in command of a division of cavalry. He served in such famous battles as Germantown.

Even though Pulaski was an able leader who also gave his own money to help the American cause, some colonists objected to fighting under a foreign commander who spoke little English. Pulaski received permission to form a command of foreign soldiers known as the Pulaski Legion. It soon became known for its courage in battle.

Pulaski and his men were sent to the South to fight British forces. While attacking a British fort at Savannah, Pulaski was

153

wounded. He died of his wounds two days later on October 11, 1779.

See Franklin County.

About Pulaski County

<u>Land and resources:</u> Most of the county has level land with over 85 percent of it used for farming. There are oak and hickory forests throughout the county, and also deposits of limestone, oil and gas, as well as sand and gravel. The Tippecanoe River splits the county into two sections.

<u>People and their work:</u> Farmers in the county raise crops such as corn and soybeans. Some also raise mint plants whose oil is used for flavoring gum, candy, and other foods. Other people work in the county's banks, restaurants, stores, and factories.

<u>Facts to remember about Pulaski County:</u> The county has acres reserved by the state to protect wildlife and provide people with beautiful areas to hike, camp, ride horseback, and enjoy other outdoor activities.

Putnam County

Named for: Israel Putman
Date organized: 1822

Israel Putnam was born in what is now Danvers, Massachusetts, on January 7, 1718. His father died when Israel was very young. Later his mother remarried and moved the family to Connecticut. As a young boy, Israel was known for his strength and daring. He could hold his own in a fight, even against two attackers. By the age of ten he had his own gun.

As an adult, Israel was a tavern keeper, soldier, and farmer. Israel almost became a legend because of all the exciting things that happened to him. During the French and Indian War he was captured by the Indians. At the last moment he was rescued from being burned at the stake by a French officer. In other adventures, Israel was shipwrecked off the coast of Cuba and served in **Pontiac's War**. He also explored the Mississippi River.

Israel Putnam believed the colonies should break from Great Britain. He joined the Sons of Liberty, a secret group of patriots who wanted war against Great Britain. It was said he was plowing his field one day when he heard the sounds of battle in the distance. He unhitched his horse, left the plow in the field, and galloped away to help the Americans fight the British.

155

Before the war ended, he had served in many battles, including the **Battle of Bunker Hill**.

Putnam's remaining years were spent on his farm in Brooklyn, Connecticut. He died there on May 29, 1790.

About Putnam County

<u>Land and resources:</u> The county has both hilly and level land with oak and hickory forests. There are deposits of sand and gravel, limestone, and gypsum. The county also has two known caves. The North Eel River runs through the county.

<u>People and their work:</u> Farmers in the county raise a large number of cattle and calves. Many also grow corn and soybeans. Other people work in the county's factories and stores. Some are employed at DePauw University in Greencastle.

<u>Facts about Putnam County:</u> Big Walnut Natural Area in the northern part of the county has many unusual types of birds, such as the great blue heron and the great horned owl. The area also has some of the largest trees in the state.

Randolph County

Named for: Uncertain
Date organized: 1818

Many of the people who settled in Randolph County probably came from North Carolina. They may have named their new county after Randolph County in their home state. But it is more likely that the county was named for Thomas Randolph. He was a general killed in the Battle of Tippecanoe.

Thomas and his twin brother, Isham, were born in 1771 in Richmond, Virginia. They were cousins of Thomas Jefferson. After graduating with honors from college, Randolph studied law. He served one term in the Virginia legislature.

Thomas Randolph married, but his young wife soon died. He then traveled to the Indiana Territory. His friend William Henry Harrison,* who was also from Virginia, appointed Randolph attorney general of the Indiana Territory.

Randolph helped to develop the growing government. But he favored slavery in the territory, a position that was unpopular with many people. When Randolph ran for Congress, he was defeated by Jonathon Jennings,** who opposed slavery. The difference over slavery created an era of bad feelings between the two men.

Randolph's temper often led him into conflict with others. He was once stabbed in the back with a dagger, and he responded by cutting his attacker's face with a pocketknife. At another time Randolph challenged a newspaper reporter to a fight after the reporter had written unpleasant things about him. Randolph was arrested and had to put up a bond, or large sum of money, promising that he would not harm the reporter.

Randolph served as prosecuting attorney for Knox and Harrison counties. When William Henry Harrison began his campaign against the Indians, Randolph offered to serve. While fighting in the campaign, he was killed by an Indian bullet.

See Harrison County.
**See Jennings County.*

About Randolph County

Land and resources: Randolph County, which lies along the Ohio border, has mostly level land with over 85 percent of it used for farming. There are some forests of oak, hickory, beech, birch, and maple. The county has deposits of sand and gravel, oil and gas, limestone, and clay. The Mississinewa River flows through the northern part of the county.

People and their work: Farmers in the county raise large crops of winter wheat and oats. Many other people work in the county's factories and in banks and health service jobs.

Facts to remember about Randolph County: Although much of the county's land is level, it has the highest point of **elevation** in the state. At Lynn, in the southern part of the county, the elevation is 1,285 feet above sea level.

Ripley County

Named for: E. L. Wheelock Ripley
Date organized: 1818

Born in Hanover, New Hampshire, in 1782, Eleazar Wheelock Ripley was named for his maternal grandfather, who founded Dartmouth College. Young Eleazar graduated from Dartmouth in 1800. After studying law and setting up a practice, he became active in politics. From 1807 to 1811 he served as a member of the Massachusetts legislature.

When war broke out between the United States and Great Britain in 1812, Ripley enlisted in the army and became a lieutenant colonel. He prepared his troops with demanding drills. In April, 1813, his troops took part in the attack on York (now Toronto), Canada. He took an active part in several other battles and was promoted to brigadier general. He was wounded in the fall of 1813 and received a gold medal from Congress for "gallantry and good conduct."

In 1820 Ripley resigned from the army and returned to law practice in Louisiana. In 1832 he was elected to the Louisiana Senate. He later served Louisiana in the nation's House of Representatives. Ripley died in 1839 while still in office.

About Ripley County

<u>Land and resources:</u> Ripley County has low rolling hills, except in the southeast, where the land is level. There are forests of oak, hickory, beech, maple, and birch. The county also has deposits of limestone as well as oil and gas. Laughery Creek flows through the county.

<u>People and their work:</u> Many of the county's farmers raise tobacco. Other people work in the county's factories, schools, and recreation areas.

<u>Facts to remember about Ripley County:</u> One of Indiana's first railroads crossed the northern part of Ripley County. The train, which ran from Lawrenceburg to Indianapolis, was pulled by horses instead of an engine.

Many of Indiana's first railroads, like the one which ran through Ripley County, went to Indianapolis. This painting shows the Union Station there in the 1850s.

Rush County

Named for: Benjamin Rush
Date organized: 1822

Benjamin Rush, a well-known doctor and signer of the Declaration of Independence, was born on a farm near Philadelphia in 1745. His father died when he was a baby, and his mother went to work in Philadelphia so Benjamin could receive an education. He attended an academy in Maryland and Princeton College. He then studied medicine in Europe and America.

Rush returned to America and became a professor. As the political unrest in the colonies grew, he took the side of the patriots. He was a member of the Continental Congress, signed the Declaration of Independence, and became an army doctor.

After the American Revolution, Rush was involved in both medicine and politics. In Philadelphia he set up the first free clinic in the United States for poor people. He was a member of the Pennsylvania convention to **ratify** the United States Constitution. He also helped shape Pennsylvania's state constitution.

Dr. Rush was one of the few doctors who stayed in Philadelphia during a yellow fever epidemic that took 4,000 lives. Rush's treatments of the sick persons, however, created arguments. He believed in taking blood from people or giving them strong laxatives to make them weak. This, he thought,

161

would also make the disease weak. Rush himself became ill but lived to treat still another yellow fever epidemic in Philadelphia.

Although some people came to think of him as a "quack," or a doctor who only pretends to have medical knowledge, Rush worked for several important causes. He helped establish the first antislavery society and the first Negro church in Philadelphia. He also joined in an effort to stop cruel treatment of the mentally ill and worked to end capital punishment. Rush died in Philadelphia in 1813.

About Rush County

Land and resources: The eastern part of Rush County has hilly land, while the western part has more level and gently sloping areas. Over 85 percent of the land is used for farming, and there are some forests of birch, maple, beech, elm, ash, and cottonwood trees. The county also has deposits of sand and gravel as well as limestone.The Flatrock River cuts through the county from north to south.

People and their work: The county's farmers grow crops such as corn, soybeans, and winter wheat. They also raise many hogs. Other people in the county have jobs in stores, banks, and factories that make such products as parts for air conditioners and refrigeration units. Some work in neighboring counties.

Facts to remember about Rush County: The county has some of the best farmland in the nation, and its farmers once produced more hogs than any other U.S. county. Wendell Wilkie, who ran for President in 1940, lived in Rushville, the county's seat.

Francis Vigo (upper left), Anthony Wayne (upper right), Marquis de Lafayette (lower left), and William Henry Harrison (lower right) all had Indiana counties named after them.

Many people visit the farm in Spencer County where Abraham Lincoln lived from 1816 to 1830. People also like to visit the state's Lake Michigan beaches, like this one in Porter County.

St. Joseph County

Named for: St. Joseph River
Date organized: 1830

There are two St. Joseph rivers in Indiana. St. Joseph County is named after the river that begins near Hillsdale, Michigan, and follows a winding course southward into Indiana. There it flows through a part of Elkhart County and into St. Joseph County. Near South Bend the river turns northward once again. After its 210-mile journey, the river empties into Lake Michigan.

The river has been a part of Indiana's history. It's name has changed through the centuries. The Potawatomi Indians called it Sag-wa-si-bi, or "mystery river," because a strange Indian appeared on its banks. To the Miami Indians it was the Sa-ke-wa-si-wi, or "coming out place." The first recorded European in the area called it the "river of the Miami." Later the French named the river for the patron saint of Canada, St. Joseph.

Perhaps the river's most famous explorer was Robert, Sieur de La Salle. On a bitter day in December, 1679, La Salle paddled down the river from Lake Michigan. He was searching for the mouth of the Mississippi River, which he had been told by the Indians could be reached by following other, smaller rivers. La Salle, with his party, reached a spot near the present-day city of South Bend.

The St. Joseph River has been traveled by Indians, French trappers and hunters, and finally settlers looking for land. Today the St. Joseph's waters are used for sport and recreation.

About St. Joseph County

Land and resources: Most of St. Joseph County has level land, about half of which is used for farming. The county has forests of oak, hickory, maple, birch, and beech. It also has deposits of sand and gravel, peat, and marl. In addition to the St. Joseph River, the county has a number of lakes.

People and their work: The county's farmers raise crops such as corn and soybeans. Some also raise mint, which is used to flavor foods. Other people in the county are employed in schools and colleges. Some work in the county's factories, which make machinery, metal products, rubber products such as raincoats, and parts for guided missiles.

Facts to remember about St. Joseph County: The county seat, South Bend, is one of Indiana's largest cities as well as the home of the University of Notre Dame. The Studebaker automobiles were built in South Bend for many years, as were Oliver tractors and other types of farm equipment.

Scott County

Named for: Charles Scott
Date organized: 1820

Charles Scott, a military hero, was born in what is now Powhatan County, Virginia. He received little schooling, but he knew a great deal about how to live in the wilderness. At the age of seventeen, Charles served under George Washington as the Revolutionary War began. He raised armies, commanded them in battle, a became a major general. Scott fought bravely until he was captured by the British. He remained a prisoner until the end of the war.

After the Revolutionary War, Scott moved to Kentucky. There he used his wilderness skills as he fought against the Indians. He served with such famous military leaders as General Arthur St. Clair and General Anthony Wayne.

In Kentucky, Scott also became involved in politics. He was active in the state government for a few years before running for a major office. He then defeated John Allen* to become Kentucky's governor from 1808 to 1812.

Charles Scott died in Clark County, Kentucky, on November 8, 1854. A county in Kentucky was named for him, as well as the county in Indiana.

See Allen County.

167

About Scott County

Land and resources: Much of Scott County is hilly with forests of oak and hickory. A little more than half of the land is used for farming. The county has deposits of limestone and dolomite. The Muscatatuck River forms the county's northern border, while Hardy Lake provides a recreation area for many people.

People and their work: Farmers in the county grow crops such as corn, soybeans, and tobacco. Other people work in the county's banks, hotels and motels, construction businesses, and factories.

Facts to remember about Scott County: In 1812 a little settlement named Pigeon Roost was attacked by Shawnee Indians. Its twenty-four residents were killed by the Indians. In the 1860s the county was the scene of one of the world's first train robberies that captured the nation's attention.

Shelby County

Named for: Isaac Shelby
Date organized: 1822

Isaac Shelby, the first governor of Kentucky, was born December 11, 1750, in Maryland. As a boy, Shelby received little schooling. But he learned how to live on the frontier, how to use a rifle, and how to be a surveyor. As a teenager, Isaac served as a sheriff in Maryland. When his family moved to Virginia, he helped his father establish a general store.

After serving in the American Revolution, Shelby moved to Kentucky. He enjoyed the beauty of that region, and he and his wife and their eleven children settled down to stay. The Shelbys called their home Traveler's Rest.

In Kentucky, Shelby began a political career. He helped to establish Kentucky's state constitution and became the state's first governor in 1792. He returned to private life for a time, but was later reelected governor.

With the outbreak of the War of 1812, Shelby worked for the appointment of William Henry Harrison* as commander of the army of the Northwest. Shelby then sent soldiers called the Kentucky Volunteers to join General Harrison in the fight with the British for control of the Great Lakes. The residents of Fort Detroit in the Michigan Territory were so grateful for the help of the Kentucky Volunteers they renamed their fort Shelby. One of Shelby's sons was killed in the war.

Shelby's friends and supporters wanted him to continue his political career and try to become Vice President of the United States. But Shelby wanted to live a private life at Traveler's Rest, where he was surrounded by his children and grandchildren. Isaac Shelby died at his home on July 18, 1826.

See Harrison County.

About Shelby County

Land and resources: Most of the land in Shelby County is level, with about 85 percent of it used for farming. There are forests of oak, maple, beech, and birch. The county also has deposits of sand and gravel, limestone, and dolomite. The Blue River cuts through the county from north to south, while the Flatrock River crosses the county's southeastern corner. The land near these rivers is hilly.

People and their work: Most farmers in Shelby County raise corn, soybeans, and hogs. Other people work in factories, in stores, and in construction jobs. Some go to neighboring counties to work.

Facts to remember about Shelby County: One of Indiana's earliest railroads ran through Shelbyville, the county seat. The railroad had only one car and was pulled by horses. Shelbyville was also home to Charles Major, who wrote best-selling novels around the 1900s.

Spencer County

Named for: Spier Spencer
Date organized: 1818

Spier Spencer, a hero in the Battle of Tippecanoe,* came to Indiana from Shelby County, Kentucky. He settled in Vincennes, but lated moved to Corydon. There he and his wife Elizabeth ran a log tavern called The Green Leaf. Spier was elected sheriff of Harrison County, and later headed the Harrison County militia.

Spencer's militia was made up of about sixty men. They dyed the cuffs of their coats or the fringes of their buckskin shirts yellow and were nicknamed the "Yellow Jackets." The Yellow Jackets acted mainly as Spencer's deputies, catching horse thieves and other lawbreakers. But in the fall of 1811, the Yellow Jackets joined William Henry Harrison's** army. It was the army's purpose to break up a growing group of Indians led by Tecumseh. The Indian headquarters was located at Prophetstown, near the present-day city of Lafayette.

On November 7, 1811, at about 4:30 in the morning, the Indians attacked Harrison's army. The Yellow Jackets were under heavy fire. Captain Spier Spencer was one of the first to be wounded. But even with injuries to both legs, he refused to leave the battle. Soon he received wounds to the head and chest. Spencer died as he was carried from the battle.

*See Tippecanoe County.
** See Harrison County.

About Spencer County

Land and resources: Spencer County is largely made up of hills and valleys. The county has forests of oak and hickory and many mineral deposits, including coal, sand and gravel, oil and gas, clay, shale, limestone, and sandstone. The Little Pigeon Creek forms the county's western boundary and Anderson River forms its eastern boundary. The Ohio River makes up the county's southern boundary.

People and their work: Spencer County's farmers raise crops such as tobacco, corn, soybeans, and hay. They also raise cattle, poultry, and hogs. Many other people go to neighboring counties to work. Others are employed in banks, recreation areas, and health services.

Facts to remember about Spencer County: Abraham Lincoln spent many of his boyhood years in the county. There are a number of memorials in the county honoring Lincoln. His mother, Nancy Hanks Lincoln, is buried here. The county also has a town named Santa Claus.

Starke County

Named for: John Stark
Date organized: 1850

John Stark, a soldier and American patriot, was born in Londonderry, New Hampshire on August 28, 1728. Stark served as a soldier both in the French and Indian War and the American Revolution. His life was filled with adventure. Once he was captured by Indians. His friends bought him back for $103, a very large sum at that time.

During the French and Indian War, John fought with Roger's Rangers. This group was noted for courage and daring. As a member of the Rangers, Stark helped capture **Fort Ticonderoga** in 1756 and later helped save **Fort William Henry** from a French attack.

At the beginning of the American Revolution, Stark raised a regiment of soldiers and served as their colonel. His regiment fought in such battles as Bunker Hill. He served with George Washington during the winter of 1776 to 1777. Stark was made a brigadier general for his part in defeating two forces from the British army led by General John Burgoyne. Stark also scored other important victories during the war.

John Stark died in Manchester, New Hampshire, on May 8, 1822.

About Starke County

Land and resources: Level land covers most of Starke County, and over 75 percent of it is used for farming. The county has hardwood forests of oak and hickory. It also has deposits of sand and gravel, peat, and clay. The Kankakee River forms much of the county's western boundary. In the southern part of the county Bass Lake provides people with a pleasant place to swim, fish, boat, or picnic.

People and their work: Starke County's farmers grow crops such as corn, soybeans, and mint, which is used to flavor foods, gums, and candies. Other people in the county work in banks, stores, or restaurants. Some work in the county's factories. Still others have jobs in neighboring counties.

Facts to remember about Starke County: The land along the Kankakee River is generally low and was once swampy. Much of the swampland has been drained and now provides fertile soil for farming. Even so, one of the county's towns was probably named for creatures that enjoy wetlands. Toto, in the central part of the county, may have been an Indian word meaning "bullfrog."

Steuben County

Named for: Baron Friedrich Wilhelm von Steuben

Date organized: 1837

Baron Friedrich von Steuben, part of a family that had produced soldiers for many generations, was born in Prussia on September 17, 1730. From the age of 14, Steuben, lived a soldier's life too. He was trained in the best army in Europe, that of Frederick the Great of Prussia. Steuben was so brave that even the king noticed him, and the young soldier became the king's special aide.

When Steuben learned of the American Revolution, he wrote to George Washington and offered his services as a volunteer. When he arrived in America, Steuben was sent to Valley Forge to join Washington's army. Using his training and skills, he began drilling the inexperienced colonial soldiers. He soon was in charge of training all the troops of the colonial army.

Steuben's job was a difficult one. The colonial soldiers had little equipment, were poorly dressed, and were often hungry. Steuben made a plan for organizing this strange army. He taught the men how to care for their guns and weapons. Under

175

Steuben's drilling and guidance the colonial rebels became soldiers who were able to meet and defeat the enemy.

When the American Revolution was over, Steuben was given a farm in New York State. In 1784 Congress gave him a sword with a gold handle and special thanks for giving the colonies his services. Baron von Steuben became a U.S. citizen and spent his remaining years at Steubenville, New York. He died there on November 28, 1794.

About Steuben County

Land and resources: The county has both level and slightly hilly land, with over 70 percent of it used for farming. In some areas there are forests that include oak, hickory, maple, beech, and birch. The county has deposits of sand and gravel, shale, and marl. It also has a number of lakes.

People and their work: Farmers in Steuben County raise corn and livestock. Other people have jobs in factories, stores, or the health care industries. Many are teachers or have jobs at schools and colleges.

Facts to remember about Steuben County: Because it has so many forests and lakes, the county is sometimes called the "Switzerland of Indiana." The county has five state nature preserves where trees, flowers, and wildlife are protected. Tri-State University is located in Angola, the county's seat.

Sullivan County

Named for: Daniel Sullivan
Date organized: 1817

Daniel Sullivan was born in what is now Pittsburgh, Pennsylvania, in 1758. At the age of nine, Daniel was captured by Indians. For the next few years, Daniel learned the skills taught to all Indian boys, including hunting and fishing. He seemed to find a new and happy life among the Indian people with whom he lived.

On a trip to Fort Pitt with the Indians, Daniel and another boy who had been captured with him were recognized by their old friends. Daniel's companion rejoiced to be returned to his family. But fifteen-year-old Daniel refused to leave the Indians, even when the whites offered a horse, a saddle, six hachets, three red blankets, and a gallon of whiskey for him. Finally Daniel agreed to stay when his relatives promised him a beaver hat!

Daniel was caught between two worlds, the Indian and the white. He did not adjust well to the world at Fort Pitt, and after about a year he returned to his Indian friends. But as an Indian he refused to fight against white people. After six years his feelings for white people brought him back to an American fort. He fought against the Indians and was wounded.

177

During the American Revolution Daniel Sullivan became a spy, scout, and guide for the colonists. While carrying a message from Vincennes (in what is now Indiana) to Louisville (in what is now Kentucky), Sullivan and his party were attacked by Indians. The Indians pleaded with Sullivan to surrender, but he refused and kept fighting. The place where Daniel Sullivan was killed became known as Sullivan's Spring.

About Sullivan County

Land and resources: Much of the county is made up of hills, except in the north and west, where there are areas of level land. Forests of oak and hickory cover some of the land, while about 60 percent of it is used for farming. The county has large deposits of coal, along with deposits of sand and gravel. The Wabash River forms the county's western boundary. In the eastern part of the county there are many lakes that have been made where coal was once mined.

People and their work: Many people in Sullivan County are farmers or work in the coal mining industry. Farmers raise corn, soybeans, and hogs. Other people work in the county's logging industry, electric power plants, and factories that make salt shakers and other plastic products. Many Sullivan County residents go to other counties to work.

Facts to remember about Sullivan County: One of the county's early residents, John W. Davis, came within one vote of running for President in 1852. He lost to Franklin Pierce, but later became the nation's ambassador to China.

Switzerland County

Named for: The country of
Switzerland

Date organized: 1814

Switzerland County was named by John Dufour, who left his home in Switzerland to search for a good place to raise grapes and make wine. Dufour arrived in Philadelphia in 1796. He journeyed as far west as St. Louis, examining the land along the Ohio and the Mississippi rivers. Finally he purchased 2,500 acres in what is now Switzerland County, Indiana.

Immediately Dufour set about the task of making a vineyard. He hired help, and with them worked all fall and winter, clearing land. By the spring of 1799 they had six acres cleared and ready for planting. Dufour chose thirty-five different kinds of grapes and planted a total of 10,000 vines.

In 1801 John's five brothers and three sisters joined him from Switzerland, bringing vines from Swiss vineyards. By 1806 the first Hoosier grape wine was ready. According to reports, 12,000 gallons were produced.

By 1814 settlers from Ohio, Pennsylvania, and New York had moved to the area surrounding Dufour's vineyard. They wanted the area, then part of Dearborn County, to be a separate county. John Dufour agreed and presented a **petition** to the Territorial Legislature in 1814. The lawmakers passed an act organizing the county. Dufour chose the county's name because the hills around the Ohio River reminded him of his former home in Vevay, Switzerland. The county seat was named Vevay.

About Switzerland County

Land and resources: Much of the land in Switzerland County is hilly, with forests of oak, hickory, maple, beech, and birch. The county has deposits of sand and gravel, oil and gas, as well as limestone. The Ohio River forms the southern and eastern borders of the county.

People and their work: Switzerland County farmers grow crops such as tobacco, oats, and hay. They also raise livestock. Other workers have jobs in the county's factories, which make leather, plastic, and metal products. About one third of Switzerland's workers have jobs outside the county.

Facts to remember about Switzerland County: Edward Eggleston, a writer born in Vevay, wrote a novel about backwoods life in southeastern Indiana during the 1830s. *The Hoosier School-Master*, as it was called, and another Eggleston novel, *The Circuit Rider*, were bestsellers and made Eggleston nationally famous. Switzerland County people try to preserve the history of their county by building stores and restaurants with a Swiss theme and staging a Swiss festival each year.

Tippecanoe County

Named for: The Tippecanoe River and the Battle of Tippecanoe

Date organized: 1826

The Tippecanoe River begins in Kosciusko County and flows through five counties, a distance of 220 miles, before it empties into the Wabash. It is a shallow, fast stream. Its stone and gravel bottom makes it good for smallmouth bass fishing. The word Tippecanoe comes from an Indian word, *Kith-tip-pe-ca-nunk* or *Ke-tap-e-kon-nong,* meaning "Buffalo fish."

The area around the Tippecanoe River was the home of many Indian tribes, including the Miami,* the Shawnee, and the Potawatomi. It was also the area where Tecumseh and his brother, the Prophet, planned a union of Indian tribes to drive white settlers from the country.

The largest battle fought on Indiana soil took place near the Tippecanoe. It was waged between the United States Army and the Indian union of Shawnee, Potawatomi, Winnebago, and Chippewa bands. The U.S. Army was under the leadership of General William Henry Harrison* and included 600 Indiana volunteers, 60 Kentucky volunteers, and 250 regular soldiers.

Harrison and his army left Vincennes in southern Indiana in September, 1811. In early November he reached the Tippe-

181

canoe River. After talking with the Indians and arranging for a peace meeting the next day, the army made camp.

At 4:15 the next morning about 700 Indians attacked the soldiers. Heavy fighting followed. Thirty-seven Americans were killed and one hundred and fifty-one were wounded before the Indians were defeated. After the battle the soldiers burned the nearby Indian village of Prophetstown.

The battle at Tippecanoe was important because it was the last major Indian effort to stop American settlement in the Northwest Territory. The Tippecanoe battlefield itself was later purchased by John Tipton.*** He gave it to the state so that it could become a memorial.

*See Miami County.
**See Harrison County.
***See Tipton County.

About Tippecanoe County

Land and resources: Level land makes up most of the county. About 80 percent of it is used for farming. There are some hardwood forests that include oak, hickory, maple, and beech. The county also has deposits of sand and gravel as well as clay. The Tippecanoe River flows into the Wabash in the northeastern part of the county.

People and their work: Farmers in the county grow soybeans, corn, and winter wheat. They also raise hogs, cattle, and poultry. Many people in the county who are not farmers are doctors, lawyers, or teachers. Others work in stores or in factories that make automobile supplies, electrical equipment, and medicines.

Facts to remember about Tippecanoe County: Purdue University is located in the county. Every summer, visitors can see the Battle of Tippecanoe staged in an outdoor theater near the battlefield. Fort Ouiatanon, once a French fort used to protect the fur trade, is located in the county and is one of Indiana's oldest historic sites.

Tecumseh worked to create a united Indian force that he hoped would defeat American troops.

Tenskwatawa, also known as the Prophet, lost the Tippecanoe battle to Harrison.

Tipton County

Named for: John Tipton
Date organized: 1844

John Tipton, a United States Senator from Indiana, was born in eastern Tennessee on August 14, 1786. When John was only seven years old, his father was killed by Indians. Life for the family was difficult, and John never went to school. Later the family moved to a home near Brinley's Ferry in Harrison County, Indiana. John split rails for fences, worked on a ferry boat, and was a hired hand on nearby farms.

When Tipton was twenty-three he joined the Harrison County Yellow Jackets, a group of sheriff's deputies who caught horse thieves and other lawbreakers. The unit was led by Captain Spier Spencer.* When the Yellow Jackets joined the army and fought at the Battle of Tippecanoe,** Spencer was killed and Tipton was elected captain on the battlefield.

After the Battle of Tippecanoe, Tipton returned home and commanded a group of rangers, who were to protect Harrison and Clark counties from Indians. John became Harrison County's first sheriff. He served Indiana as a surveyor, a member of the state government, and a United States Senator. Tipton also bought and sold large amounts of land during his career. He helped plan the building of canals to connect Indiana's rivers and gave the state the old Tippecanoe battlefield to make into a memorial.

John Tipton married twice. His first wife died after only two years of marriage. He later married Matilda Spencer, daughter of Spier Spencer. She died in 1839. John Tipton died two months later at the age of 52.

*See Spencer County.
**See Tippecanoe County.

About Tipton County

Land and resources: Level land makes up most of Tipton County, and nearly all of it is used for farming. There are some forests of elm, ash, oak, hickory, and cottonwood trees. There are also deposits of sand and gravel.

People and their work: Tipton's farmers grow crops such as corn, soybeans, and oats. They also raise hogs and smaller crops of apples and tomatoes. A large number of people who are not farmers have jobs in neighboring counties. Others work in Tipton's stores, offices, and factories, one of which processes and packs seeds for farmers.

Facts to remember about Tipton County: Large swamps once covered large sections of land in the county. These swamps were drained, creating unusually rich farmlands. The excellent soil is the county's most important natural resource.

Union County

Named for: Uncertain
Date organized: 1821

When Indiana became a state, there were no guidelines about how many counties should be formed. Thus, as new counties were created, their boundaries often overlapped those of existing counties. People often urged Indiana lawmakers to change boundaries of older counties so that new counties could be made. This caused unrest in the state government on the subject of forming new counties and changing boundaries of older ones.

Wayne County and Franklin County, once much larger than they are today, were counties when Indiana became a state in 1816. In 1818 Fayette County was formed, drawing from both Franklin and Wayne counties. Angry feelings grew between the people living in these counties.

In 1820 Fayette County leaders proposed to extend the county's boundaries to the eastern edge of the state. The plan was turned down. Instead, a new county was created east of Fayette County. Wayne, Fayette, and Franklin all contributed area to the new county.

The name Union was selected for the new county. There are several thoughts on why the name Union was chosen. Some think that the word "union" suggested a feeling of patriotism for the United States. Other people believe it may have been named for the town of Union, already established on the east bank of Hanna's Creek. The most likely reason for its name is that it was to bring a feeling of union and harmony between the three counties of Wayne, Franklin, and Fayette.

About Union County

Land and resources: Rolling hills cover much of the land in Union County. About 80 percent of the land is used for farming. Some is covered with forests of oak, hickory, cottonwood, elm, and ash. The county has deposits of sand and gravel. Part of the large Brookville Lake lies in the county.

People and their work: Farmers in the county raise hogs and crops such as corn and soybeans. Other people work in stores and factories. Many have jobs in other counties.

Facts to remember about Union County: One of Indiana's smallest counties, Union's eastern boundary helps form the state line between Indiana and Ohio. The large reservoir called Brookville Lake stretches between Union County and Franklin County and gives residents a fine recreation area.

Vanderburgh County

Named for: Henry Vanderburgh
Date organized: 1818

Henry Vanderburgh was born in Troy, New York, in 1760. At the age of sixteen he became an officer in the Continental Army. He served with honor until the end of the American Revolution. After the war Henry traveled to the Northwest Territory. In 1791 he was appointed justice of the peace and a judge for Knox County, which was formed even before the Indiana Territory. Later Vanderburgh became a judge for the entire Indiana Territory. He held that office until his death on April 12, 1812. He also served on the board of trustees of Vincennes University.

About Vanderburgh County

Land and resources: Vanderburgh County has both level and hilly land. About half of the land is used for farming.There are many forests of oak and hickory. The county also has deposits of sand and gravel, oil and gas, as well as clay. The Ohio River forms the county's southern border.

<u>People and their work:</u> Farmers in the county grow corn, soybeans, and mushrooms. They also raise livestock. Other people work in stores or factories that produce such items as refrigerators, agricultural equipment, and furniture. Some have professional jobs in education, law, or medicine.

<u>Facts to remember about Vanderburgh County:</u> Evansville, the county seat, is the transportation center of southwestern Indiana. It is served by trucks, trains, and boats on the Ohio River. The county is also the site of Angel Mounds. Ancient Indians built these mounds between 1200 and 1400 A.D.

This 1936 photo shows one of the mounds at Angel Mounds. The Indians had a large building on the flat part of the mound.

Vermillion County

Named for: The Vermillion River
Date organized: 1824

There are three rivers in small, narrow Vermillion County. They are the Wabash, the Big Vermillion, and the Little Vermillion. Both Vermillion rivers flow into the Wabash, but the county is named for the Big Vermillion. The Big Vermillion River begins in Illinois and flows into the Wabash River near Newport, the county seat.

The Indians were the first to name the river. They called it Osanamon, which means "yellow-red paint." They used the red substance called vermilion from the river for war paint and other decorations. Changing the Indian name to their own language, the French called the river Vermillion Jaune.

Indians made their homes at the mouth of the Vermillion River until the early 1800s. The tribes there were the Kickapoo and the Piankasha. The power of the Indians in that area was challenged by William Henry Harrison.* In 1811 Harrison and his men camped along the Wabash near the mouth of the Vermillion on their march to the Tippecanoe. The army built a small **blockhouse**, and some of the men remained there to receive supplies on the Wabash River.

About Vermillion County

Land and resources: Vermillion County is made up of both hilly and level land. About 70 percent of the land is used for farming. Some of the land is covered with oak and hickory forests. The county has deposits of coal and clay as well as sand and gravel. The Wabash River forms the county's eastern boundary while Illinois makes up the western boundary.

People and their work: Farmers in the county raise such crops as corn and soybeans. They also raise livestock. Other people in the county work in factories and stores and in construction. Many go outside the county for jobs.

Things to remember about Vermillion County: The county's best known citizen was Ernie Pyle. Pyle joined the American soldiers in World War II and wrote newspaper stories about the war. Millions of Americans read his columns and learned what the war was really like. Pyle lost his life in the war.

Vigo County

Named for: Francis Vigo
Date organized: 1818

Francis Vigo was born on the island of Sardinia in the Mediterrean Sea in 1740. He left his home as a youth and enlisted in the Spanish army. He was sent to Havana, Cuba, and later shipped on to New Orleans. In New Orleans Francis resigned from the Spanish army and began trading furs with the Indians. He and his partner became rich.

Francis Vigo met George Rogers Clark* at Kaskaskia, a French fort along the Mississippi River in what is now southwest Illinois. Clark asked Vigo to carry papers to an American officer at Fort Sackville in Vincennes. When Vigo arrived at the fort he was taken prisoner by British General Henry Hamilton. To save himself and the information he was carrying, Vigo chewed up and swallowed the papers Clark had given him. He was released by the British and returned to Kaskaskia, telling Clark all he had seen and heard.

During the American Revolution, Vigo loaned great sums of money to Clark and the Americans. When the war was over, Vigo settled in Vincennes. But the funds he loaned the American government were not repaid. When Vigo died at the age of 96 he was a poor man. His funeral expenses amounting to $20 could not be paid until the government settled with Vigo's family forty years later. By that time the interest on his $8,616 loan to the government amounted to $41,000!

See Clark County.

About Vigo County

Land and resources: Most of the land in Vigo County is level. A little more than half of it is used for farming. There are also forests of oak and hickory. The county has sand and gravel, oil and gas, limestone, and large coal deposits. The Wabash River forms the county's western border.

People and their work: Vigo County farmers raise corn, soybeans, and winter wheat. There are also a number of farmers who raise nursery and greenhouse products, such as flowers, trees, and shrubs. Many people in the county are teachers, lawyers, doctors, and dentists. Others work in stores or factories.

Facts to remember about Vigo County: Vigo County's seat, Terre Haute, means "high land." It was named by the French. From its beginnings, it was a transportation center for riverboats and wagon trains loaded with settlers moving west. Today it is important for coal mining and other industries. It is also the home of Indiana State University.

Wabash County

Named for: The Wabash River
Date organized: 1835

The Wabash is Indiana's longest river. It stretches over 500 miles from its beginnings in western Ohio. The river enters Indiana in Jay County, flows northwest to Huntington, and then west to Lafayette. From there it bends south and forms the boundary between Indiana and Illinois. The Wabash flows into the Ohio River in the southwest corner of Indiana.

Some of the land along the Wabash was once the home of ancient people who hunted, fished, and gathered shellfish along its banks. Later inhabitants along the river were the Miami Indians. To them the Wabash was the boundary that marked the end of the great forest and the beginning of the prairie. The Miami Indians named the water Wa-bah-shik-ki, which meant "white or bright water." French trappers and traders who came later used the word Ouabache as they attempted to change the Indian name to French.

Perhaps the first Frenchman to see the Wabash was the explorer named Robert, Sieur de La Salle. About 1670 La Salle followed the Ohio River, probably to the point where it is joined by the Wabash.

The present-day Wabash River is no longer white or bright as in the days when Indians were the region's only inhabitants. Its waters are muddy with **silt** from the farms located along its banks. Still, many Hoosiers think of the beauty of the Wabash, especially when they listen to the song, "On the Banks of the Wabash." The song was written by an Indiana composer, Paul Dresser, and his brother, Theodore Dreiser, in 1897. It was popular all over the nation for many years.

About Wabash County

Land and resources: Nearly all of the land in Wabash County is level. About 80 percent of it is used for farming. There are forests of oak, elm, hickory, ash, and cottonwood trees. The county also has deposits of sand and gravel, oil and gas, marl, and limestone. The Wabash and Eel rivers run through the county. There are also a number of lakes there, including areas of the Mississinewa and Salamonie Lakes.

People and their work: Farmers in the county raise large numbers of cattle and calves, hogs, and poultry. They also grow corn and soybeans. Other people have jobs in the county's stores, health service programs, and factories.

Facts to remember about Wabash County: Wabash, the county seat, was one of the first cities in the world to be lighted by electricity. Country singing star Crystal Gayle was born in Wabash County.

Warren County

Named for: Joseph Warren
Date organized: 1827

Joseph Warren was born at Roxbury, Massachusetts, on June 11, 1741. He was the oldest of Joseph and Mary Warren's four sons. When he was fourteen, Joseph entered Harvard College. After graduation he became a teacher. But Warren's teaching career was short. He returned to his studies, this time to become a doctor.

Warren's experience as a doctor led him to still another career. He met John Adams while giving Adams a shot to prevent smallpox. Through his meeting with Adams, Warren became very interested in politics. He gave up his medical practice to devote his time to public service.

Before the American Revolution broke out, Warren was actively involved with the American patriots. He attended meetings, worked on committees, and gave speeches. He headed important organizations in the colonies. On April 18, 1775, it was Joseph Warren who sent Paul Revere and William Dawes on their famous rides to warn the patriots that British soldiers were approaching Concord.

Warren was asked to serve as a physician during the war, but he desired more active duty. He was to be a major general, but before his papers arrived, he began serving as a regular soldier. Warren never became a major general. On June 17, 1775, he was killed by the British at the Battle of Bunker Hill. He was remembered by those who knew him as a kind and gentle person.

About Warren County

Land and resources: Warren County has both level land and gently rolling hills. Most of the land is used for farming. Some is covered with hardwood forests of oak and hickory. The county has deposits of clay, sand and gravel, coal, and shale. The Wabash River forms much of the county's southeastern border.

People and their work: Farmers in Warren County grow crops such as soybeans and corn. They also raise hogs, poultry, and cattle. Other people in the county have jobs in stores, hospitals and other health care centers, and factories. Many go to neighboring counties to work.

Facts to remember about Warren County: In 1838 over 800 Potawatomi Indians were forced out of Indiana to a reservation in Kansas. They had to make the trip on foot, traveling along the Wabash through Williamsport, the county seat. The Trail of Death, as it is sometimes called, lasted about two months. About 150 Potawatomi died along the way.

Warrick County

Named for: Jacob Warrick
Date organized: 1813

Little is known about the life of Jacob Warrick. Warrick, a friend of William Henry Harrison,* served in the Indiana army at the Battle of Tippecanoe.** Early in the battle he was badly wounded and was taken to a safe area to have his wounds treated. Warrick insisted on walking back and leading his men in battle even though he was near death. He died before the battle ended.

*See Harrison County.
**See Tippecanoe County.

About Warrick County

Land and resources: Warrick County is made up of both hilly and level land. There are many forests of oak, hickory, cottonwood, beech, and maple. The county is rich in coal deposits. It also has deposits of sand and gravel, oil and gas, limestone, clay, and shale. The Ohio River forms the county's southern boundary, while Little Pigeon Creek makes up its eastern boundary.

<u>People and their work:</u> Many of the county's people work in the coal mining industry and in stores and factories. Others have jobs in the health care field. Warrick's farmers raise crops such as corn and soybeans. Some grow apples, sweet corn, and tomatoes.

<u>Facts to remember about Warrick County:</u> Abraham Lincoln sometimes walked to Boonville, the Warrick County seat, to hear a lawyer named John A. Brackenridge give excellent speeches in court. Many runaway slaves also came to the county as they crossed the Ohio River and landed at the mouth of Little Pigeon Creek. During the Civil War some Confederate scouts raided several stores in the town of Newburgh. This became known as the first Confederate attack north of the Ohio River.

Washington County

Named for: George Washington
Date organized: 1814

George Washington was born on February 22, 1732, in Westmoreland County, Virginia. His father died when George was eleven. The youngster was sent to live with an older half brother, Lawrence, at his plantation called Mount Vernon. Lawrence taught George how to fish, hunt, and plant.

George had little formal education compared with his older brothers. He had a natural talent for geography and mathematics and became a surveyor. In 1748 he traveled west to the Blue Ridge Mountains as an assistant surveyor.

When Lawrence died an early death, George became the owner of Mount Vernon. He also took over his brother's job as an officer in the Virginia army. During the French and Indian War, Washington became known for his ability as a military leader. Some of his adventures were published in a book called *The Journal of Major George Washington,* which also helped make him famous.

In 1759 Washington married Martha Custis, a widow with two children. During the next fifteen years he became one of the wealthiest men in Virginia. He was also one of the largest landholders in all the colonies.

When the Revolutionary War began, the Continental Congress named Washington head of the Continental Army. That army was new and untrained. Keeping the men from quitting and finding them food and clothing was as big a job as teaching them to become soldiers who could win battles.

After the war Washington was anxious to return to a peaceful life at Mount Vernon. But he was called on to head the **Constitutional Convention** in Philadelphia. When the Constitution was **ratified,** he was elected the first President of the United States. He served two terms as President and then retired to Mount Vernon, where he died in 1799. At his funeral it was said that Washington was "first in war, first in peace and first in the hearts of his countrymen."

About Washington County

Land and resources: Hilly land makes up much of Washington County. About 60 percent of the land is used for farming, and there are forests of oak and hickory. The county has deposits of limestone and gypsum as well as oil and gas. There are at least fifty-eight caves in the county. The Blue River and the South Fork of the Blue River begin in the county. The East Fork of the White River and the Muscatatuck River make up the county's northern border.

People and their work: Washington farmers raise tobacco, corn, hay, and oats. Some grow fruits and vegetables, such as apples, melons, tomatoes, and sweet corn. Many also raise cattle. Other people in the county work in stores, restaurants, banks, and factories.

Facts to remember about Washington County: Washington County was one of the first fifteen counties in the Indiana Territory. Salem, the county seat, was an early center for roads and railroads. It was a stop on the Lafayette and Jeffersonville Turnpike and on the New Albany and Salem line, a railroad that stretched all the way from the Ohio River to Lake Michigan.

This drawing of one of the trains that traveled on the New Albany and Salem line appeared on the advertising of the railroad company in 1860.

Wayne County

Named for: Anthony Wayne
Date organized: 1811

Anthony Wayne, a Revolutionary War hero, was born in 1745 in Waynesborough, Pennsylvania. As a young man, he managed the family's business after the death of his father. When the American Revolution began, Wayne raised an army of volunteer soldiers and fought in many important battles. He received a medal from Congress as well as the nickname Mad Anthony for his daring acts.

Wayne had a political career as well as a military one. He served as a lawmaker in Pennsylvania both before and after the Revolutionary War. In 1792 President George Washington sent Wayne to the Northwest Territory, where the Indians were fighting to stop American settlement.

After carefully training an army for Indian fighting in the wilderness, Wayne marched into areas of the Ohio region where Indian power was strongest. Indians made several attempts to attack the marching army but with little success. The Indians called Wayne the chief who never sleeps. He also earned names such as The Wind, The Hurricane, and Black-snake because of the power of his army.

Wayne was able to destroy Indian armies and villages in what is now Ohio and Indiana. He drove the Indians out and built forts in what is now western Ohio. Wayne's greatest victory was the Battle of Fallen Timbers, south of the present city of Toledo, Ohio. This was a huge loss to the Indians and forced them to give up most of their land in the Ohio region. After his victory at Fallen Timbers, Wayne and his army marched southwest along the Maumee River destroying Indian villages along their way into Indiana Territory. When the army reached the Miami Indian town of Kekionga, they destroyed it also and built a fort named Fort Wayne.

When Wayne left the Indiana fort he met with Indian leaders at Fort Greenville in what is now Ohio. A treaty was signed and Wayne became a hero for bringing peace to the Northwest Territory. But his life as a daring soldier took a toll on him. He died from the effects of old war wounds on December 15, 1796.

About Wayne County

Land and resources: Wayne County, which lies along the Indiana-Ohio border, is made up of level and slightly hilly land. Much of the land is used for farming, and there are forests of oak and hickory. There are deposits of sand and gravel, oil and gas, limestone, and dolomite. The West Fork of the Whitewater River flows through the county.

People and their work: Wayne farmers grow crops such as oats, hay, corn, soybeans, and mushrooms. Other people have jobs in professional fields, such as teaching, medicine, or law. Many work in stores and in factories that makes such products as automobile parts, school buses, and tools. Some people have jobs in the county's large rose-growing industry.

Facts to remember about Wayne County: The county seat of Richmond was nearly destroyed in 1968 as the result of a terrible gas explosion and fire. Richmond has since been rebuilt and is the home of Earlham College. The northern part of the county is the home of Levi and Catherine Coffin. Their home housed nearly 2,000 runaway slaves before the Civil War. The house is known as the Grand Central Station of the Underground Railroad.

Levi Coffin was an important leader in the Underground Railroad and helped many slaves escape to Canada.

Wells County

Named for: William Wells
Date organized: 1837

When he was about eleven years old, William Wells was captured by the Indians and taken from his home in what is now Louisville, Kentucky. He was taken to Turtle Village on the Eel River in the territory that was to become Indiana. There he was adopted by an Indian family and named Apekonit, meaning "wild potato," perhaps because of his red hair.

William was raised as an Indian, and as he grew to be a warrior, his name was changed to Black Snake. A strong bond grew between him and Chief Little Turtle. When William was about twenty years old, he married Sweet Breeze, daughter of Little Turtle.

Wells was fierce in battle against enemy Indians and whites. He was put in charge of 300 warriors in a battle against General Arthur St. Clair and about 2,000 American soldiers near what is now the Indiana-Ohio border. It was said that Wells killed or injured so many soldiers with his tomahawk that by the end of the battle he was so tired he could no longer raise his arm.

Since so many of the soldiers in the battle with St. Clair were from Kentucky, Wells was upset. He began to wonder if any of the men he killed might have been his relatives. He decided to return to Kentucky to visit his family. While he was there, he joined a group of scouts made up of white men who had been raised by Indians.

It was the hope of both Wells and Little Turtle that the knowledge Wells learned by living with both Indians and whites could help bring peace. Wells became a valuable scout for General Anthony Wayne.* He fought against Indians in the Battle of Fallen Timbers and acted as an **interpreter** in the Treaty of Greenville (see Wayne County). These actions did not break his tie with Little Turtle. Wells returned to Fort Wayne and continued to be friends with Little Turtle. When the chief traveled to sign treaties, Wells went with him.

William Wells, or Blacksnake, lived only a few weeks longer than his Indian friend, Little Turtle. Wells was leading a group of Miami Indians from Fort Wayne to Fort Dearborn (Chicago) when they were attacked by Potawatomi Indians. He died on August 15, 1812.

See Wayne County.

About Wells County

Land and resources: Most of the land in Wells County is level. About 85 percent of the land is used for farming, but there are also forests of maple, oak, beech, hickory, and birch. The county has deposits of sand and gravel, peat, and limestone. Both the Wabash River and the Salamonie River cross the county.

People and their work: Farmers in the county raise crops such as corn, oats, hay, and winter wheat. They also raise dairy cattle, hogs, and poultry. Other people work in hospitals, health centers, banks, and factories, one which makes snack foods. Some have jobs in nearby counties.

Facts to remember about Wells County: Wells County was slow to grow because settlers feared attacks by Chief Black Hawk and his men. Black Hawk, whose village was in Illinois, often made trips to Ontario, Canada, to trade with the British. He and his followers often attacked settlers along the way because they believed the treaties were unfair and the land really belonged to the Indians.

Printers once made engravings or sketches after famous paintings and then reproduced them in books, newspapers, or other printed material. This engraving of Little Turtle was made from a painting by Gilbert Stuart, a famous American artist.

White County

Named for: Isaac White
Date organized: 1834

Isaac White was born in Prince William County, Virginia, shortly after the beginning of the American Revolution. Isaac's father was killed in the war, leaving his wife, Isaac, and two other children. Isaac and his brother remained at home until their mother remarried. Both in their twenties, the boys objected to their mother's marriage and left home, traveling to Indiana Territory in the early 1800s.

In Vincennes, Isaac met and married Sallie Leech. He also became a friend of the William Henry Harrison* family. Harrison gave White a job heading a government **salt works** in Illinois. White held the job for five years.

White became a friend of Joseph Hamilton Daveiss.** The two joined the forces of Harrison to fight the Indians. Even though White was a private and Daveiss was a major, the two were close enough to exchange swords when they left Vincennes on September 26, 1822, to march to Tippecanoe. White was killed in the battle, and Daveiss was also killed. Both men were buried in a single grave, and their names appear on a monument on the battleground.

*See Harrison County.
**See Daveiss County.

About White County

<u>Land and resources:</u> Level land covers nearly all of White County. About 90 percent of the land is used for farming. The county has forests of oak and hickory. It also has deposits of oil and gas, limestone, dolomite, and shale. The Tippecanoe River flows through the county from north to south. Along its path are two large lakes, Lake Shafer and Freeman Lake.

<u>People and their work:</u> Farmers in White County grow large crops of corn and soybeans. They also raise hogs and poultry. Other people in the county have jobs in recreation areas and health service industries. Many work in factories making products that range from toys and puzzles to truck trailers.

<u>Facts to remember about White County:</u> White County is sometimes called the summer playground of the Midwest. It has a large amusement park along with many areas for boating, swimming, fishing, and other water sports.

Whitley County

Named for: William Whitley
Date organized: 1838

William Whitley, a cousin of George Rogers Clark,* was born in Virginia on August 17, 1749. He moved to Kentucky at the age of twenty-six and lived at Boonesborough until he built Whitley's Fort in southeastern Kentucky. Whitley had many experiences with Indians. He rescued white captives and led a group of men to fight Indians who attacked Kentucky towns. He was also sent to Indian villages on peace missions.

In the War of 1812, Whitley volunteered to be part of a Kentucky army organized by Governor Shelby.** The group traveled north to Canada. There Whitley was killed in 1813 in the famous Battle of the Thames, which helped the Americans win the war against the British.

*See Clark County.
**See Shelby County.

About Whitley County

<u>Land and resources:</u> The northern part of Whitley County has low, rolling hills. In the southern half the land is nearly level. Over 80 percent of the land is used for farming. Some is covered with forests of maple, oak, beech, hickory, and birch. There are also deposits of sand and gravel as well as peat. The Eel River flows through the county on its journey to the Wabash.There are also a number of lakes in the county.

<u>People and their work:</u> Farmers in Whitley County grow large crops of hay, oats, and winter wheat. Many other people work in the county's stores and factories.

<u>Facts to remember about Whitley County</u>: Thomas R. Marshall lived in Columbia City, the county seat. Marshall was governor of Indiana in the early 1900s. He also served as Vice President of the United States under President Woodrow Wilson.

County	County Seat	Size (square miles)	Population
Adams	Decatur	340	30,600
Allen	Fort Wayne	659	295,300
Bartholomew	Columbus	409	66,300
Blackford	Hartford City	166	15,500
Boone	Lebanon	423	38,600
Brown	Nashville	312	13,500
Carroll	Delphi	372	19,900
Cass	Logansport	414	40,500
Clark	Jeffersonville	376	92,000
Clay	Brazil	360	25,000
Clinton	Frankfort	405	31,300
Crawford	English	307	10,600
Daviess	Washington	432	28,800
Dearborn	Lawrenceburg	364	37,000
Decatur	Greensburg	373	23,800
Dekalb	Auburn	364	33,900
Delaware	Muncie	392	124,600
Dubois	Jasper	429	35,700
Elkhart	Goshen	466	145,200
Fayette	Connersville	215	28,300
Floyd	New Albany	150	63,100
Fountain	Covington	398	19,000
Franklin	Brookville	385	20,600
Fulton	Rochester	369	19,900
Gibson	Princeton	490	34,400
Grant	Marion	415	78,700
Greene	Bloomfield	546	31,400
Hamilton	Noblesville	398	94,300
Hancock	Greenfield	307	46,800
Harrison	Corydon	337	29,700
Hendricks	Danville	409	76,000
Henry	New Castle	394	51,800
Howard	Kokomo	293	86,600
Huntington	Huntington	366	36,300
Jackson	Brownstown	513	37,300
Jasper	Rensselaer	561	27,900
Jay	Portland	384	22,700
Jefferson	Madison	363	31,100
Jennings	Vernon	378	23,900
Johnson	Franklin	321	83,200
Knox	Vincennes	520	42,000
Kosciusko	Warsaw	540	64,800
Lagrange	LaGrange	380	27,800
Lake	Crown Point	501	506,600
LaPorte	LaPorte	520	109,000

Lawrence	Bedford	452	43,500
Madison	Anderson	453	133,800
Marion	Indianapolis	396	780,000
Marshall	Plymouth	444	41,000
Martin	Shoals	339	11,000
Miami	Peru	369	39,200
Monroe	Bloomington	385	101,400
Montgomery	Crawfordsville	505	35,700
Morgan	Martinsville	409	54,500
Newton	Kentland	401	15,400
Noble	Albion	413	37,100
Ohio	Rising Sun	87	5,400
Orange	Paoli	408	19,000
Owen	Spencer	386	17,100
Parke	Rockville	444	16,800
Perry	Cannelton	382	19,400
Pike	Petersburg	341	13,900
Porter	Valparaiso	418	131,000
Posey	Mt. Vernon	409	27,600
Pulaski	Winamac	436	13,600
Putnam	Greencastle	482	30,000
Randolph	Winchester	454	29,800
Ripley	Versailles	447	25,400
Rush	Rushville	408	18,900
St. Joseph	South Bend	459	241,000
Scott	Scottsburg	291	21,100
Shelby	Shelbyville	413	40,200
Spencer	Rockport	400	20,600
Starke	Knox	309	22,700
Steuben	Angola	308	26,300
Sullivan	Sullivan	452	21,200
Switzerland	Vevay	223	7,600
Tippecanoe	Lafayette	502	123,800
Tipton	Tipton	260	16,819
Union	Liberty	162	6,900
Vanderburgh	Evansville	236	167,600
Vermillion	Newport	260	18,300
Vigo	Terre Haute	405	110,400
Wabash	Wabash	398	36,500
Warren	Williamsport	391	8,900
Warrick	Boonville	391	47,100
Washington	Salem	516	22,800
Wayne	Richmond	404	73,400
Wells	Bluffton	370	25,500
White	Monticello	506	24,500
Whitley	Columbia City	336	26,900

Indiana's Warmest Counties

1. Gibson
2. Pike
3. Posey
4. Vanderburgh
5. Warrick
6. Spencer
7. Perry
8. Harrison
9. Floyd
10. Clark
11. Jefferson
12. Ohio

Indiana's Coldest Counties

1. Porter
2. La Porte
3. St. Joseph
4. Elkhart
5. La Grange
6. Steuben
7. Noble
8. De Kalb
9. Newton
10. Jasper
11. Pulaski
12. Fulton
13. Whitley
14. Allen
15. Wabash
16. Benton
17. Warren
18. Tippecanoe
19. Randolph

Indiana Counties With The Most Snowfall Each Winter

1. Lake
2. Porter
3. La Porte
4. St. Joseph
5. Elkhart
6. Starke
7. Kosciusko
8. Noble
9. Whitley
10. Blackford

Indiana Counties With The Most Rainfall Each Year

1. La Porte
2. Brown
3. Lawrence
4. Ripley
5. Ohio
6. Orange
7. Washington
8. Warrick
9. Spencer
10. Perry
11. Crawford
12. Harrison

Glossary

Allies. People, groups, or nations who have a common interest or cause.

Ambassador. A person who represents his or her government in another country.

American Revolution. A war in which American colonies fought for and won their independence from Great Britain.

Apprentice. A person who works for another in order to learn a trade.

Architects. People who draw plans for buildings.

Artillery. Large guns too heavy to carry.

Battle of Fallen Timbers. A battle fought in 1794 between American troops and several Indian tribes in the western Great Lakes area. The American victory forced the Indians to give up much land in Ohio and Indiana.

Battle of New Orleans. Although the War of 1812 had ended, the news traveled slowly and the British attacked American troops in New Orleans. The Americans defeated the British in this unnecessary battle.

Bifocal glasses. Eyeglasses that have two parts. One part is to help see things close at hand and another part to help see things far away.

Black Hawk War. Several battles fought in 1832 between U.S. soldiers and some of the Sauk and Fox tribes who did not want to leave their Illinois lands.

Blockhouse. A fort-like house usually built of logs with special holes for guns so that people inside can shoot at attackers.

Bluffs. High steep banks.

Boston Tea Party. Before the American Revolution Boston citizens dumped 342 chests of tea into the harbor to protest the high taxes placed on them by Great Britain.

Brandywine. An important battle of the American Revolution that took place in 1777 near Philadelphia. British troops defeated American soldiers led by George Washington.

Bunker Hill. An early battle in the American Revolution that took place on Breed's Hill close to Boston. Although the skilled British soldiers won, the Americans showed great strength.

Chautauqua. A place in western New York State noted for its fine cultural programs.

Chief Justice of the Supreme Court. The judge who is in charge of the highest court in the land.

Civil War. The war fought from 1861-1865 between the northern and the southern United States over the question of slavery.

Clan. A large group of Indians within a tribe that have some relationship with each other through their religious beliefs.

Colonial Army. The general army of the American colonies.

Commissioner. A person chosen to run a department, often in a government.

Congress. The highest lawmaking body of our nation which includes both the **Senate**

and the **House of Repre-
sentatives**.

Constitution. A written
document which establishes the
basic laws of a nation or state and
the rights of its people.

Constitutional Convention.
A meeting of **delegates** for the
purpose of writing a constitution
for a state or nation.

Continental Congress.
Delegates from the thirteen
colonies who ran the American
colonies during the American
Revolution.

Coral reef. A ridge of rock
made up of millions of hardened
seashells.

Cumberland Mountains. Part
of the Appalachian Mountains,
located largely in Kentucky and
Tennessee.

**Declaration of Indepen-
dence.** A statement made by the
thirteen American colonies in
1776 declaring them to be free
from the rule of Great Britain.

Delegate. A person selected to
speak and act for his or her
group.

District attorney. A lawyer
who works for the people or the
government in a certain area.

Document. An important printed
or written record used to prove
something.

Dolomite. A kind of **limestone**.

Duel. A fight between two
people with weapons and special
rules.

Elevation. The height of
something. The elevation of land

is measured according to its
height above the sea.

Fort Ticonderoga. A British
fort in what is now northern New
York State that was used as a base
in making raids on French troops
in Canada.

Fort William Henry. A fort
built by the British near Lake
George in what is now northern
New York State to stop the
French from taking over the area.

French and Indian War. A
war lasting from 1754 to 1763 in
which the French and their Indian
allies fought the British for
control of North America. The
French lost nearly all of the land
east of the Mississippi River.

French Revolution. The war
in France which began in 1789 by
taking the power away from the
king but ended in 1799 with the
rule of Napoleon who was even
more powerful than a king.

Frontier. The part of a settled
country that lies next to an
unsettled part.

Germantown. A part of
Philadelphia where George
Washington unsuccesssfully
attacked British forces during the
American Revolution.

Glaciers. A huge masses of ice
and snow that move slowly down
a mountain or across land until
they melt.

Governor. The person elected to
be the head of a state.

Great Compromisor. A name
given to Henry Clay for saving
the young United States three

times when arguments nearly divided it.

Gypsum. A chalky mineral used in making plaster.

House of Representatives. A lawmaking branch of **Congress** which is made up of a number of representatives from each state, depending on the **population** of the state.

Immigrants. People who move to a foreign country to make their home.

Interpreter. A person who explains the meaning of another language.

Iroquois Indians. A group of tribes living in an area south of the St. Lawrence River and Lake Ontario. The Iroquois tribes spoke the same language, shared a system of government, and had many trained warriors.

Land agent. A government employee who has control over buying and selling public lands.

Legislature. A body of elected people who make or change laws.

Limestone. Rock that is used to make building stones or is ground up to be used in cement or other products.

Log rolling. The sport of rolling a log rapidly in the water by running on it.

Louisiana Territory. Land reaching from New Orleans to the Canadian border and from the Mississippi River to the Rocky Mountains. The U.S. purchased this land from Spain in 1803.

Marl. A type of earth or soil used as a fertilizer.

Marshall. An officer of a U.S. Court with a job like a sheriff.

Mayor. The head of the goverment in a city or town.

Michigan Road. An early Indiana road that ran from southwestern Michigan, through Indianapolis, to Madison on the Ohio River.

Michigan Territory. A section of the **Northwest Territory** that was created in 1805. Boundaries changed many times before the state of Michigan was formed.

Militia. A group of people who are not regular soldiers, but who have some military training and form an army in times of trouble.

Minister. A person who represents his or her government in another country and who ranks one step below an **ambassador**.

Moat. A deep wide ditch dug around a castle to keep enemies away.

Moravian Indians. Indians from the Delaware tribe who lived peacefully and followed the Christian faith as practiced by Moravians, a group of Protestants who came to America from Moravia in eastern Europe.

Northwest Territory. An area of land stretching north from the Ohio River to Canada and west from Pennsylvania to the Mississippi River.

Orator. A good public speaker.

Orchids. A plant that grows in warm regions and has very pretty flowers.

Peat. A mass of partly rotted plants and grass formed in marshes. It is used for fertilizer, but can also be dried and used for fuel.

Penn, William. A Quaker leader who started the colony of Pennsylvania.

Pewter. A gray metal made of tin mixed with lead, brass, or copper.

Politician. A person that runs for or holds a public office.

Pollution. The act of putting harmful materials into the environment.

Pontiac's War. A series of attacks made on the British at Fort Detroit by the Indians under the leadership of Pontiac.

Population. The total number of people living in a place, such as a country or city.

Postmaster. A person in charge of a post office.

Prophet. A Shawnee Indian leader in the Indiana area who believed Indians should turn away from white people's customs and return to a true Indian life. His Indian name was Tenskwatawa.

Prosecutor. A lawyer who carries out legal actions against a person.

Proverbs. Old sayings that tell something wise.

Ratify. To approve of some formal action.

Rebels. People who fight against the people in control.

Salt works. A building or buildings where salt is made.

Sandstone. A kind of rock formed mainly of sand.

Secretary of State. The official chosen by the President of the U.S. to head the Department of State which is in charge of our country's relations with other countries.

Secretary of War. The official chosen by the President of the U.S. to make sure the nation has good armed forces and weapons. Today this official is known as the Secretary of Defense.

Senate. A body of government made up of two representatives from each state. This body, along with the **House of Representatives**, is known as **Congress** and has the power to make and change laws.

Senator. One of two people elected from each state to serve in the U.S. Senate. A senator can also be an official serving in the senate of a state government.

Shale. A type of rock which is formed by clay and can easily be split.

Silt. Fine soil and sand carried by moving water.

Sioux Indians. A group of seven related Indian tribes who spoke the same language and lived on America's prairies and plains.

Soldier of fortune. A military person ready to serve anywhere for money.

Speaker of the House. The leader in the **House Of Representatives**.

Stalagmites. Icicle-shaped formations that look like rock and rise from the floor of some caves.

Stamp Act. A tax introduced in the American colonies by the British to help cover the cost of defending the colonies against the French armies and the Indians. The people opposed the tax and it was ended in 1767.

Strip mines. Mines in which minerals are dug from open pits or trenches instead of underground.They are often called surface mines.

Supreme Court. The highest or most important court in the U.S.

Surveyor. A person who measures the exact boundaries of a section of land.

Teamster. A person whose work is hauling loads with a team of horses.

Treaty of Alliance. An agreement that brought the French to the side of the Americans during the American Revolution.

Treaty of Paris. An agreement signed in 1783 by leaders of the new United States and Great Britain that marked the end of the American Revolution.

Trustees. People who take care of the property or business of others.

Underground Railroad. A term used to describe networks of people in the North who helped slaves reach safety in Canada.

Utility company. A company that provides some public service, such as producing electricity or offering bus transportation.

Valley Forge. A camp near Philadelphia where George Washington and his army spent the winter of 1777-78. Many soldiers died because there was not enough food or warm clothes.

Wabash and Erie Canal. Finished in 1853, this canal joined Lake Erie to Evansville on the Ohio River via the Wabash River. Its 468-mile course made it the longest canal in the United States.

Wagon master. A person leading a group of vehicles on a trip.

War of 1812. Fought in North America between the U.S. and Great Britian between 1812 and 1815.

West, Benjamin. An American artist who settled in London and taught other artists. The events and leaders of his day were often the subjects of his paintings.

West Indies. A group of islands in the Atlantic Ocean, south of the U.S.

Wilderness Road. A pathway used by pioneers traveling west through the **Cumberland Mountains**.

Yorktown. A town in Virginia where the last important battle of the American Revolutionary War took place.

Index

Counties are listed in alphabetical order in the text and are not included in the index unless there are additional references.

Adams, John, 7- 8, 41, 91, 196
Adams, John Quincy, 7-8, 33
Allen, John, 10-11, 167
American Revolution, 7, 24-25, 29-31, 32, 36, 38, 43-44, 47, 55, 71, 73, 92, 94, 106, 107, 119, 129, 131, 133, 153, 155, 167, 175, 196, 201
Amish, 9, 54, 110
Anderson, Chief, 49, 118
Appleseed, Johnny, 12
Bartholomew, Joseph, 13-14
Benton, Thomas, 15-16
Bird, Larry, 140
Blue River, 39, 76, 94, 76, 84, 102, 170
Blackford, Isaac, 17
Black Hawk War, 14, 208
Boone, Daniel, 19-20, 59, 79, 138
Branigan, Roger, 102
Brown, Jacob Jennings, 22
Buffalo Trace, 52
Burr, Aaron, 74, 117
Carroll, Charles, 24-25
Cass, Lewis, 26-27
Catarack Falls, 142
caves, 39-40, 79, 140, 201
Civil War, 16, 146, 148, 199
Clark, George Rogers, 29-31, 59, 84, 106, 192, 211
Clay, Henry, 33-35
Clinton, DeWitt, 36-37
coal, 35, 62, 68, 106, 124, 142, 146, 152, 172, 178, 191, 193, 197
Coffin, Levi & Catherine, 205
Conner, William, 49

Constitution, State, 25
Constitution, U.S., 64, 117, 161, 201
Corydon, 79, 81, 171
Crawford, William, 38-39
Daviess, Joseph, 41-42, 209
Davis, John W., 178
Dean, James, 70
Dearborn County, 43-44, 179
Dearborn, Henry, 43-44
Decatur, Stephen, 45-46, 115
Declaration of Independence, 25, 97, 161
deKalb, Baron Johann, 47-48
Delaware Indians, 49-50
dolomite, 18, 25, 28, 31, 46, 88, 102, 126, 168, 170, 204, 210
Dreiser, Theodore, 195
Dresser, Paul, 195
Dubois, Toussaint, 51
Duesenberg automobiles, 48
Dufour, John, 179-180
Eel River, 126, 156, 195, 206, 212
Elkhart River, 53, 99, 136
Erie Canal, 12, 27
Farming & farm crops. *See* About — facts at the end of each chapter.
Fayette County, 55-56, 186
Floyd, Davis, 59-60
Floyd, John, 59
Fort Dearborn, 43, 207
Fort Detroit, 10, 27, 30, 169
Fort Ouiatanon, 183
Fort Sackville. *See* Vincennes
Fort Wayne, 10-12, 58, 204, 207
Fountain, James, 61-62
Franklin, Benjamin, 63-64, 153
Franklin County, 63-64, 186
French and Indian War, 38, 137, 155, 173
Fulton, Robert, 65-66
Gibson, John, 67-68, 94, 101
Grant, Moses, 69-70
Grant, Samuel, 69-70
Greene, Nathaniel, 71-72

Grissom, Virgil (Gus), 116
Hamilton, Alexander, 22, 73-74
Hamilton, Henry, 30, 192
Hancock, John, 75-76
Hanover College, 81, 98
Harmer, Josiah, 61
Harrison, Benjamin, 78
Harrison County, 77-78, 158, 171, 184
Harrison, William Henry, 42, 49, 68, 77-78, 141, 157, 169, 171, 190, 198, 209
Haynes, Elwood, 86
Hendricks, William, 81-82
Henry, Patrick, 33, 83-84
Howard, Tilghaman, 85-86
Huntington, Samuel, 87
Indianapolis, 120
Indiana Territory, 67, 77, 99, 151, 188, 202
Indians, 13, 19-20, 29, 38-39, 49-50, 53, 61, 67, 77-78, 118, 122, 125-126, 177-178, 181-182, 189, 190, 203-204, 206-207. *See* also Miami, Shawnee, & Potawatomi
Industry, 12, 16, 18, 28, 31, 35, 37, 44, 48, 50, 52, 54, 56, 60, 70, 72, 76, 86, 91, 102, 108, 112, 114, 118, 120, 130, 138, 140, 146, 150, 166, 178, 180, 183, 185, 189, 205, 210
Iroquois River, 93, 134
Jackson, Andrew, 15, 27, 89-90, 99, 149
Jackson, Michael, 112
Jasper, William, 92-93, 119, 133-134
Jay, John, 94
Jefferson, Thomas, 44, 96-97, 117, 143, 157
Jennings, Jonathon, 99-100, 157
Johnson, John, 101
Kankakee River, 93, 112, 114, 134, 174

Knox County, 101, 105-106, 15ᵇ, 188
Knox, Henry, 105-106
Kosciusko, Thaddeus, 56, 107-108
Lafayette, Marquis de, 55, 109
Lake Michigan, 111-112, 165
LaSalle, Robert, 134, 137, 165, 194
Lawrence, James, 115
limestone, 9, 18, 23, 25, 28, 31, 35, 37, 39, 46, 50, 64, 68, 70, 72, 79, 86, 88, 97, 102, 116, 118, 120, 126, 128, 132, 134, 142, 146, 154, 158, 160, 162, 168, 170, 172, 180, 193, 204, 208, 210
Lincoln, Abraham, 172, 199
Little Calumet River, 112
Little Turtle, 125, 206-207
Livingston, Robert, 65-66
Madison, James, 8, 36, 117-118, 127
marl, 50, 66, 122, 176, 195
Marion County, 112, 119-120
Marion, Francis, 72, 119-120
Marshall, John, 44, 121-122
Marshall, Thomas, 212
Maumee River, 12, 62, 204
Miami Indians, 11, 88, 125, 137, 181, 194, 207
Michigan Road, 28, 37, 46
Michigan Territory, 27, 169
Mississinewa River, 50, 70, 158
Monroe, James, 44, 127-128
Montgomery, Richard, 129
Morgan, Daniel, 131-132
Muscatatuck River, 91, 97, 100, 168, 201
National Road, 56, 82
Natural resources. *See About* — feature at the end of each chapter. *See also* Coal, Dolomite, Limestone, Marl, Peat, & Shale.
New Harmony, 152

, 133-134

⌐5

⌐itory, 12, 27, 29-
⌐, 125, 141, 182,

⌐ver, 39, 44, 56, 60, 79,
⌐8, 135, 137-138, 146,
⌐⌐2, 172, 179-180, 194, 198
Owen, Abraham, 141
Parke, Benjamin, 101, 143
Patoka River, 52, 68, 140, 148
peat, 9, 11, 25, 48, 66, 70, 74, 76,
84, 86, 110, 114, 118, 122,
134, 174, 208, 212
Perry, Oliver Hazard, 145-146
Pigeon River, 110
Pike, Zebulon, 147-148
Porter, David, 149-150
Porter, Gene Stratton, 136
Potawatomi Indians, 10, 53,
122, 181, 197, 207
Putnam, Israel, 155-156
Pyle, Ernie, 191
railroads, 25, 28, 37, 46, 72, 100,
160, 170, 202
Richardville, Jean Baptiste, 85
Riley, James Whitcomb, 76
Ripley, E. L. Wheelock, 159
Rush, Benjamin, 77, 161-162
St. Mary's River, 11
St. Joseph River, 11, 165-166
Salamonie River, 88, 95, 208
shale, 23, 25, 34, 36, 39, 72, 81,
86, 88, 91, 97, 102, 110, 116,
130, 132, 172, 176, 197, 210
Shelby, Isaac, 169-170
slaves & slavery, 34, 95, 99,
101, 148, 151-152, 157
Shawnee Indians, 31, 168, 181
Spencer, Spier, 142, 171-172
Starke, John, 173
Steuben, Friedrich Wilhelm von,
175-176
Studebaker automobiles, 166
Sullivan, Daniel, 177-178

Switzerland County, 69, 179-180
Tecumseh, 77-78, 171, 181
Tippecanoe, Battle of, 13, 42,
51, 78, 142, 157, 181-182,
184, 198, 209
Tippecanoe River, 66, 108, 122,
154, 182, 210
Tipton, John, 14, 184-185
Underground Railroad, 95, 148,
205
Vanderburgh, Henry, 101
Vermillion River, 190
Vigo, Francis, 30, 101, 192-193
Vincennes, 30, 51, 99, 106, 192
Vincennes University, 101, 144, 188
Voorhees, Daniel W., 62
Wabash & Erie Canal, 12, 27, 28
Wabash River, 9, 12, 28, 42, 51-
52, 88, 126, 137, 142, 152,
178, 190-191, 193-195, 197, 208
War of 1812, 10-11, 15, 22, 27,
45, 90, 117, 145, 148, 149,
159, 169, 211
Warren, Joseph, 196-197
Warrick, Joseph, 198
Washington, George, 26, 37, 47,
55, 73, 94, 97, 107, 118, 151,
167, 175, 200-201, 203
Wayne, Anthony, 13, 26, 77, 125,
151, 167, 203-204
Wayne County, 186, 203-205
Wells, William, 206-207
White, Isaac, 209-210
White River, 50, 68, 74, 91, 94,
102, 106, 116, 118, 120, 124,
132, 148, 201
Whitewater Canal, 64
Whitewater River, 44, 56, 64
Whitley, William, 211
Wilkie, Wendell, 162
Wright, Orville, 84
Wright, Wilbur, 84